DOROTHY STRACHEY

(1866–1960) was one of ten children of Sir Richard Strachey and Jane Maria Grant. She was born in Clapham, London, a member of an accomplished Victorian family, the most famous of which was her younger brother, Lytton. She was educated privately and then, in 1882, followed her sister Elinor to school at Fontainebleau. Marie Souvestre (fictionalized as the Mlle Julie of *Olivia*) was headmistress there, as she was of the London school at which Dorothy Strachey later taught. Two years after Dorothy's departure for Fontainebleau, the Strachey family removed to Lancaster Gate.

In 1903, when she was nearly forty years old, Dorothy Strachey married the French painter, Simon Bussy, whom she met through her family. They lived at Roquebrune in the South of France and had one daughter. In 1918 she was introduced to André Gide, became his chief English translator and established a close friendship which lasted until his death thirty years later. Matisse was also a good friend.

Dorothy Strachey published only two books: *Olivia* appeared in 1949, under the pseudonym "Olivia" (taken from the name of a sister who died in infancy). It was acclaimed for its presentation of emotions in a girls' school and later became a cult French film starring Simone Simon. A year later a very different, although equally original book was published: *Fifty Nursery Rhymes, with a Commentary on English Usage for French Students*.

Dorothy Strachey's daughter died tragically in 1960 and her own death swiftly followed.

VIRAGO
MODERN
CLASSIC

NUMBER
268

OLIVIA

I

OLIVIA

WITH A NEW AFTERWORD BY
SUSANNAH CLAPP

Virago

Published by VIRAGO PRESS Limited 1987
41 William IV Street, London WC2N 4DB

First published in Great Britain by The Hogarth Press Ltd 1949
Copyright The Hogarth Press Ltd 1949
Afterword Copyright © Susannah Clapp 1987

British Library Cataloguing in Publication Data
Olivia
    Olivia.—(Virago modern classics).
    Rn: Dorothy Bussy   I. Title
    823'.914[F]   PR6003.U64

ISBN 0-86068-667-1

Printed in Great Britain by Cox & Wyman Ltd.
of Reading, Berkshire

TO THE BELOVED MEMORY
OF
V. W.

''L'on n'aime bien qu'une seule fois : c'est la première. Les amours qui suivent sont moins involontaires.''

LA BRUYÈRE

INTRODUCTION

I HAVE occupied this idle, empty winter with writing a story. It has been written to please myself, without thought of my own vanity or modesty, without regard for other people's feelings, without considering whether I shock or hurt the living, without scrupling to speak of the dead.

The world, I know, is changing. I am not indifferent to the revolution that has caught us in its mighty skirts, to the enormity of the flood that is threatening to submerge us. But what could I do? In the welter of the surrounding storm, I have taken refuge for a moment on this little raft, constructed with the salvage of my memory. I have tried to steer it into that calm haven of art in which I still believe. I have tried to avoid some of the rocks and sandbanks that guard its entrance.

This account of what happened to me during a year that I spent at school in France seems to me to fall into the shape of a story—a short, simple one, with two or three characters and a very few episodes. It is informed with a single motive, tends to a single end, moves quickly and undeviatingly to a final catastrophe. Its truth has been filtered, transposed, and, maybe, superficially altered, as is inevitably the case with all autobiographies. I have condensed into a few score of pages the history of a whole year when life was, if not at its fullest, at any rate at its most poignant—that year when every vital experience was the first, or, if you Freudians object, the year when I first became conscious of myself, of love and pleasure, of death and pain, and when every reaction to them was as unexpected, as amazing, as *involuntary* as the experience itself.

I know the difficulties that surround such an enterprise. I know, for instance, how careful the adjustment must be before the necessary, dry skeleton of fact can be clothed with the

warm, round, living flesh of youth, with colour and movement. I know, on the one hand, that the creature may become lean and hard, emotion withering from its bony
structure, or, on the other, for want of that structure, it may
lose its strength and purity and collapse into the amorphous
deliquescence of sentimentality.

How should I hope to succeed in such an attempt? Why
should I resist the desire to make it?

*   *   *   *   *

Love has always been the chief business of my life, the only
thing I have thought—no, felt—supremely worth while, and
I don't pretend that this experience was not succeeded by
others. But at that time, I was innocent, with the innocence
of ignorance. I didn't know what was happening to me. I
didn't know what had happened to anybody. I was without
consciousness, that is to say, more utterly absorbed than was
ever possible again. For after that first time there was always
part of me standing aside, comparing, analysing, objecting:
"Is this real? Is this sincere?" All the world of my prede-
cessors was there before me, taking, as it were, the bread out
of my mouth. Was this stab in my heart, this rapture, really
mine or had I merely read about it? For every feeling, every
vicissitude of my passion, there would spring into my mind a
quotation from the poets. Shakespeare or Donne or Heine
had the exact phrase for it. Comforting, perhaps, but en-
raging too. Nothing ever seemed spontaneously my own.
As the blood dripped from the wound, there was always part
of me to wa·ch with a smile and a sneer: "Literature! Mere
literature! Nothing to make a fuss about!" And then I
would add, "But so Mercutio jested as he died!"

And there were not only the poets to poison the sources of
emotion, there were the psychologists, the physiologists, the
psycho-analysts, the Prousts and the Freuds. It was deeply

interesting, this withdrawal of oneself from the scene of action, this lying in ambush, waiting and watching for the prowling beasts, the nocturnal vermin, to come creeping out of their lairs, to recognize this one and that, to give it its name, to be acquainted with its habits—but what was left of oneself after this relinquishing of one's property? Wasn't one a mere field where these irresponsible animals carried on their antics at their own free will? Irritation, disgust, cynicism and scepticism are bred of such thoughts—the poisonous antidotes of the poison of passion. But the poison that works in a girl of sixteen—at any rate in the romantic, sentimental girl I then was—has no such antidote, and no previous inoculation mitigates the severity of the disease. Virgin soil, she takes it as the South Sea islanders took measles—a matter of life and death.

How should I have known indeed, what was the matter with me? There was no instruction anywhere. The poets, it is true (for even then I frequented the poets), had a way of talking sometimes which seemed strangely to illuminate the situation. But this, I thought, must be an illusion or an accident. What could these grown-up men and women with their mutual love-affairs have in common with a little girl like me? My case was so different, so unheard of. Really no one had ever heard of such a thing, except as a joke. Yes, people used to make joking allusions to " school-girl crushes". But I knew well enough that my "crush" was not a joke. And yet I had an uneasy feeling that, if not a joke, it was something to be ashamed of, something to hide desperately. This, I suppose, was not so much a matter of reflection (I did not think my passion was reprehensible, I was far too ignorant for that) as of instinct—a deep-rooted instinct, which all my life has kept me from any form of unveiling, which has forbidden me many of the purest physical pleasures and all literary expression. How can one bathe without undressing, or write without laying bare one's soul?

But now, after many years, the urgency of confession is upon me. Let me indulge it. Let me make my offering on the altar of—absence. The eyes that would have understood are closed. And besides, it is not my soul but that of a far away little girl of sixteen.

One more oblation to the gods! May they grant me not to have profaned a rare and beautiful memory!

MY reserve, my recoil from all exhibitionism, was no doubt also a matter of heredity and upbringing. Which of us at home ever alluded to feelings or ever attempted to express them? But I don't doubt we had them as strong as other people. We were a Victorian household, and, in spite of an almost militant agnosticism, attached without the smallest tinge of scepticism or hypocrisy to the ideals of the time: duty, work, abnegation, a stern repression of what was called self-indulgence, a horror and a terror of lapsing from the current code. My father, who was a man of science and passed his time in investigating with heroic patience and the strictest independence of judgment one or two of the laws of nature, would not have dreamt for a moment of submitting the laws of ethics to the same scrutiny. My mother, from whom all her children inherited an ardent love of letters, and who read me aloud *Tom Jones* when I was fifteen (not that I understood one-tenth of it, utterly unenlightened as I was to the physical side of human nature) and who knew most of the Elizabethans more or less by heart, had the most singular faculty of keeping experience at bay. It was her abounding vitality, I think, that made her enjoy the blood and savagery of those outrageous authors. But she admired them from behind a wall of principle and morality which kept her absolutely safe from coming into any dangerous contact with their violence. And her own vitality, no doubt, never troubled her. Married at eighteen, and the mother of thirteen children, she was, I imagine, completely unaware of her senses. For a person who was so plunged in literature she was strangely devoid of psychology and strangely unconscious of persons. She never had a notion of what any of us children were doing or thinking, and intrigues of the most obvious and violent nature might be, and indeed often were, carried on under her very nose without her having the smallest suspicion of them. Her love of poetry was part no doubt of her sensibility to music. It was because of his sound that she reluctantly forgave Milton his abominable doctrines and learnt *Paradise Lost* by heart. But I think her chief passion in life was public affairs. Allied by birth and marriage to the aristocracy of Anglo-Indian families, the daughter and wife of great administrators, a profound interest in the craft of statesmanship was inherited in her blood and fostered by all the circumstances of her life.

I am trying to explain that though my home was very rich in intellectual influences of many sorts, there was in it a curious, an almost anomalous lack—an insufficient sense, that is—of humanity and art. With all her love of literature and music and painting, with all her vivid intelligence, my mother, I think, never felt them otherwise than with her mind. She was perhaps incapable of the mystical illumination. To speak on a lower plane, she surrounded herself with ugly objects; her furniture, her pictures, her clothes, were chosen, not without care but without taste; she was incapable of discriminating food or wine. Though we lived in the solid comfort which befitted our exact station in life, the sensual element was totally lacking from our upbringing. I remember becoming aware of this by comparing my mother with her only sister, our aunt E., who had none of my mother's mental capacity, but who was sensitive to art to the very finger-tips of her beautiful hands, and successfully created about herself an atmosphere of " ordre et beauté, luxe, calme et volupté". No; it was not only the unavoidable confusion and restrictions imposed upon a family of ten children which made our home so different. It was something much more fundamental than that.

But those missing elements which I think my childhood instinctively craved for were not to be given to me until a good deal later—until perhaps too late—when their assimilation was not possible without a profound upheaval and perhaps a permanent intoxication of my whole being.

When I was about thirteen, my mother sent me to a boarding-school which had a considerable reputation at the time and happened to be situated near to where we lived, in a London suburb which still preserved the charm of Georgian houses, spacious gardens, spreading cedar-trees, and flowering bushes. This school was kept by an eminent lady belonging to the Wesleyan persuasion. Before sending me there, my mother honourably explained our atheistical views and asked Miss Stock to give her word not to attempt to convert me. She did so and conscientiously kept it. She never spoke of religion to me personally, but I lived in a stifling atmosphere of it. I had the oppressive feeling of being an outcast, a pariah; I felt the astonishment and reprobation of my three bedroom companions when I heroically got into bed without first kneeling down by my bedside and saying or pretending to say my prayers. I was liable during my first term or two to be asked by an elder girl at any turn of a garden path whether I didn't love Jesus, which embarrassed me horribly. I assisted at prayers, at Bible classes. I went to chapel twice a day on Sundays. I heard incessant talk about our Saviour's blood, the dreadful necessity of saving one's soul, the frightful abysses into which one might fall at any moment if one didn't fly to hide oneself in the Rock of Ages. These people seemed to be beset on every side by "temptations"; they lived in continual terror of falling into "sin". Sin? What was sin? Evidently there loomed in the dark background a mysterious horror from which pure-minded girls must turn away their thoughts, but there were dangers enough near at hand which made it necessary to walk with extreme wariness—pitfalls, which one could hardly avoid without the help of God. I had to do without that, but I was very wary and naturally conscientious. Even so, one never could tell. There was the dreadful crime of "acting a lie", so hard to discern, so easy to commit. If you said you had read a book and had not looked out the meaning of every word you did not understand, there you were! A special Bible-class was convened, you were publicly told that you were "half mentally, morally and spiritually dead", and your companions were asked to pray for you. This did not happen to me personally, but such episodes made me violently indignant and extremely nervous. I should have disliked being held up to public reprobation. I should have still more disliked being expelled, and I lived in a state of continual terror. The fact that after a year or two I found a friend did not diminish my terrors—on the contrary —but it helped me to endure them. We discovered—how did we discover—after what innumerable feelers and cautious explorations of the ground, did we discover, that we were both "agnostics"? Lucy, moreover, had the credit of having become one on her own initiative. Ah! what a heavenly relief! Here was someone who rebelled like oneself, who read Shelley in secret too, who understood when one said Prometheus was greater than Christ. And then still more boldly, we ventured further; we talked of still more dangerous subjects—of love, of marriage. Should we love? Should we marry? Our heroes? Our ideals? And that extraordinary, alluring, forbidden mystery that we sensed lying at the back of all grown-up minds, what was it? We knew dimly we should never understand anything till we understood that. But oh! how innocent, how ignorant we were! How undirected, how misdirected our curiosity! How far from discovering the right track, of even suspecting its existence! But even so, we knew that our conversations were extremely perilous, to be indulged in only with the utmost precautions. We felt like two conspirators and trembled with terror if a mistress came upon us unexpectedly. Had she overheard us? Surely she had overheard us. We could see it in her face. Our consciences were loaded with guilt. If a special Bible class was convened, we went to it with knocking knees and frightful apprehensions.

We escaped, however. The end of my time was reached without disaster, and when Miss Stock bade me good-bye, she said, looking over her spectacles with the mild benevolence that characterized her in the intervals of special Bible classes:

"I am afraid, my dear, you haven't been very happy here. Can you tell me why? Is there anything you have had to complain of?"

"No! oh, no! No!"

II

I WAS rather more than sixteen when my mother decided to take me away from Miss Stock's and send me for my "finishing" to a school in France. There was one already chosen to hand, kept by two French ladies whom my mother had met several years earlier when she was staying in a hotel in Italy, and who had remained her friends ever since.

Mademoiselle Julie T—— and Mademoiselle Cara M—— were dim figures flitting occasionally through my childhood, barely distinguishable from each other, but invested in a kind of romance from the fact of their foreign nationality. They sometimes came to stay with us a little in the holidays. They nearly always sent me a child's French book on New Year's day. Starting with *Les Malheurs de Sophie*, we progressed gradually through several volumes of Erckmann-Chatrian up to *La Petite Fadette* and *François le Champi*, with one lurid and delightful interruption to dullness in the shape of a novel by Alphonse Daudet arranged for young people. Thanks to my mother and a French nursery-maid, I knew French pretty well, that is I understood it when spoken and could read it fluently; but time was too precious to be wasted on French books, so that the only ones I read were my New Year presents, and those only as a matter of duty and politeness. At Miss Stock's, the French lessons, given by a deadly Mademoiselle, were a torture from which I took refuge as best I could in depths of agreeable abstraction, only coming to the surface for a moment when it was my turn to translate two or three lines of *L'Avare* or of whatever the classic might be we were spending that particular term in stumbling through.

The new school—Les Avons it was called—was situated in one of the loveliest parts of a great forest and within easy reach of Paris. It was delightful setting off for the first time abroad. I travelled with a party of other girls, some new and some old, under the conduct of the two ladies, "*ces dames*", as it was the fashion to call them. I can't remember much of the journey, except the excitement of it.

The school was a small one, consisting of not more than thirty girls, English, American and Belgian, and a staff of German, Italian, English and French mistresses, a music mistress, and so forth.

For the first time in my life I was given a delightful little bedroom entirely to myself, and I remember it was in that room that I first looked at myself in the glass—a proceeding for which the strictest privacy is necessary, and for which, to tell the truth, I had never felt much inclination. I was beginning the new life in very different circumstances from the old. Here, I was not going to be a pariah, a goat outside the pale of salvation, and looked at with suspicion and misgiving by the Wesleyan sheep gathered safely inside it. On the contrary, I was starting, I felt, with the sympathy of the authorities and the respect of my companions, the precious daughter of a highly revered friend; and if, thought I, there is such a friendship between the French ladies and my mother, it must be that they know her "views" and possibly share them.

"And who is that tiny thing like a brownie?" I asked next morning, as I watched a curious little figure tripping and bustling down the long broad passage.

"Oh, that's Signorina, the Italian mistress. She's on Mademoiselle Julie's side."

"And just think!" said someone else, "the German mistress is a *widow*!"

"Yes, and *she's* all for Mademoiselle Cara!"

Curious words! I didn't pay much attention to them, taken up as I was for the first few days by all the novelty around me, by the kind of disorder that reigned, by the chatter and laughter, by the foreign speech, by the absence of rules, by the extraordinary and delicious meals, by an atmosphere of gaiety and freedom which was like the breath of life to me.

It was the term that begins in spring and ends in summer, and I felt indeed as if I were coming to life with the rest of the world. The grip of a numbing winter was loosened, the frozen ground had thawed, the sun was shining, the air was soft, violets and primroses were pushing up their heads in the woods. The woods lay just on the other side of the road; when we went out for our walks, as soon as we had crossed it, we were allowed to break out of file and run about as we chose, pick flowers or play games. How beautiful the woods were! How different this was from those crocodile walks along the suburban, villa-lined roads round Stockhome, where we were not allowed to forget for a single moment that we were young ladies, but must walk in step and never fall out and not talk much, though talking was the only way of amusing oneself, for there was nothing about us that we cared to look at.

On that first morning walk, my companion was a lively, pretty girl called Mimi; she took with her on a lead a big St. Bernard dog who belonged to the school and whom she had special charge of. As soon as we got into the woods, she set him free, and the great creature rushed and bounded and tried to knock us down, and we laughed and shouted and were happy.

But though I enjoyed my walk, I wasn't sorry to go in. The first week at a new school is a busy one; curriculum to be talked over, time-tables to be arranged, names and faces to be learnt. Though a new girl, I at once took my place among the elder pupils. I knew French better than a great many of them; I was to attend the visiting professors' lectures and Mlle Julie's literature lessons. (Mlle Cara, I discovered, gave no lessons.) I was to begin Italian and go on with German and Latin; I was to be allowed to give up mathematics.

So far, Mlle Julie and Mlle Cara remained, as far as I was concerned, on their Olympian heights. I had very little to do with them and only distinguished one from the other by saying to myself that Mlle Julie was the more lively and Mlle Cara the kinder. One evening, my friend Mimi, the girl with the dog, said to me: "Mlle Julie has gone to Paris and Mlle Cara wants us to go and have coffee with her in her *cabinet de travail*. Go up now. I've something I must do, but I'll be there in a moment."

I went upstairs, quaking a little, for I remembered the terrifying solemnity of my visits to Miss Stock's private sitting-room. But this, I thought, will probably be different. I hoped so.

Mlle Cara's *cabinet de travail* was on the first floor, almost next door to my own bedroom and just opposite the "ladies' " apartment on the other side of the passage. I knocked at the door and was told to come in. Mlle Cara was lying on a sofa, looking very pretty and invalidish, I thought. Frau Riesener was bending over her, arranging a shawl over her feet. As I came in, I heard Mlle Cara say: "No, no. No one cares how ill I am." Then she turned to me with a smile:

"Ah! There's Olivia. Come in, dear child. Sit down beside me and tell me what news you have from your dear Mamma."

Her voice was low, sweet and caressing, her manner all gentleness, all sympathy. She and Mlle Julie, having known me from my childhood, always said "tu" to me. I liked it. There was something, I thought, very lovely in this habit of the French language which gives it an added grace, tenderness, *nuance*, sadly lacking in English, with its single use of "you".

Frau Riesener left the room almost at once, and when a

minute or two later Mimi appeared, we were soon employed in half a dozen little ways. One of us had to fetch the eau-de-Cologne, the other soak a handkerchief and help the sufferer put it on her forehead to relieve the migraine; one had to fan her for a little, the other tuck up her shawl, which had slipped. But she was so grateful for all these little services that we enjoyed doing them and felt busy and happy. Then we had to serve the coffee and look in a cupboard for the box of chocolates; then Mimi was told to show me the album of school photographs. It was the most recent ones that I enjoyed looking at most, for among the many faces of old girls there were some of girls I could recognize as being still here. But it was an old girl's face that attracted me most. It stood out among the others, not for its beauty, for it was almost plain, but for its expression. I had never seen a face, I thought, so frank, so candid, so glad and so intelligent. But I couldn't analyse what charmed me so.

"Who is that?" I asked.

"Oh, Laura. Laura ——" answered Mimi, and she said the name of a celebrated English statesman. "Yes, his daughter; she left last term."

After that, as the pages turned, it was her face I looked for in the groups, and exclaimed with pleasure as I found it:

"Laura! There's Laura!"

"Do you admire her?" asked Mlle Cara. "For my part, I think she's downright ugly. No elegance. No grace. Always so dowdily dressed. But, of course, she has inherited brains."

Mlle Cara herself figured in all the photographs, graceful enough and languid, with a group of the smallest girls sitting at her feet.

"And Mlle Julie?" I asked. "Why is she never there?"

"Oh, she hates being photographed. It's a mania."

And so the evening came to an end. It had been unlike any

experience I had ever had of school and slid away very pleasantly, but—but—had I been altogether at my ease, hadn't I left Mlle Cara's *cabinet de travail* with a curious little sensation of discomfort?

As we walked away down the long passage together, Mimi put her arm in mine.

"Mlle Cara didn't like Laura," she said. "She was Mlle Julie's favourite."

III

I HAD been at Les Avons about a week, when one evening
after dinner, it was announced that Mlle Julie was going to
read to us.

Signorina came running up to me with sparkling eyes. She
was almost as young as I was and I never looked upon her as a
governess or a superior.

"Oh, Olivia mia, *chè piacere!* You'll like it. I know you
will."

We collected in the big music-room, dressed in our evening
frocks, with or without needlework, as we preferred. I was
surprised and relieved to find there was no compulsion. After
we had taken our seats, little Signorina flitted in and out
among us, visiting those who were sewing and giving
them advice, help, admiration or scorn. I came in for the
latter.

"Not like sewing!" she cried. "Great lazy one! Come
and look at mine!"

She took me up to a little stool which was placed close
behind the tall straight armchair, evidently reserved for Mlle
Julie, and showed me her own piece of embroidery, so delicate,
so filmy, so dainty, made of such exquisite lawn and adorned
with such tiny stitches, that I exclaimed:

"Oh, but I'm not a fairy!"

As we were laughing together, Mlle Julie came in; she gave
Signorina a glance as she passed.

"Little vanity!" she said, and went on to her chair.

Signorina turned scarlet, took up her work with a dejected
air and was just going to sit down on her stool, when Frau
Riesener came in.

"Mlle Cara wants you to make her tisane, Mademoiselle

Baietto," she said. "You're the only person who makes it properly."

"Oh," said Signorina, "but I asked her before dinner whether she would be wanting it, and she said she wouldn't."

"Well," said Frau Riesener, "she wants it now."

Signorina cast an appealing glance at Mlle Julie, who looked at her gravely and said:

"Go, my child."

Then, as Signorina went reluctantly out, she took up her book and began turning over the pages. In the meantime, I had slipped back to my own seat at the other end of the room.

"I am going to read you Racine's *Andromaque*," said Mlle Julie, "but before I begin, I'll ask you a few questions. Has anybody here ever heard of Andromaque?"

Apparently nobody ever had. At any rate there was a silence.

"Come, come," she said, "you can't all be as badly educated as that."

After another pause, I plucked up my courage and piped out:

"Hector's wife."

"Yes. And who was Orestes' father?"

I answered this too to her satisfaction. (Hadn't I browsed upon Pope's Homer since the age of twelve and eked it out with reading innumerable tales of Greek mythology?)

She went on with her questions and I answered them all until it came to Hermione.

"And Hermione?" she asked.

"I have never heard of Hermione."

"Ah!" she said, "Well, to-night you shall hear of her, and I hope never forget her. But as you've answered so well, come here and sit beside me."

She beckoned me up and made me take poor little Signorina's stool close to her elbow. Then, after lecturing us for a minute on the importance of mythology, she rapidly explained the situation at Pyrrhus's court, took up the book and began:

"*Oui, puisque je retrouve un ami si fidèle . . .*"

*   *   *   *   *

I have often wondered what share Racine had in lighting the flame that began to burn in my heart that night, or what share proximity. If she hadn't read just that play or if she hadn't called me up by chance to sit so near her, in such immediate contact, would the inflammable stuff which I carried so unsuspectingly within me have remained perhaps outside the radius of the kindling spark and never caught fire at all? But probably not; sooner or later, it was bound to happen.

There was a table in front of her with a lamp on it which cast its light on her book and her face. I, sitting beside and below her, saw her illuminated and almost in profile. I looked at her for the first time as I listened. I don't know which I did more thirstily—looked or listened. It suddenly dawned upon me that this was beauty—great beauty—a thing I had read of and heard of without understanding, a thing I had passed by perhaps a hundred times with careless, unseeing eyes. Pretty girls I had seen, lovely girls, no doubt, but I had never paid much conscious attention to their looks, never been particularly interested in them. But this was something different. No, it was not different. It was merely being awakened to something for the first time—physical beauty. I was never blind to it again.

Who can describe a face? Who can forbear trying to? But such descriptions resolve themselves into an inventory of items. As item: a rather broad face, a low forehead, dark

hair with a thread or two of grey in it, parted in the middle,
gently waving on the temples and gathered up into a bunch
of curls at the back of the head. A curious kind of hair-
dressing which I have never seen except in pictures or statues.
The features were regular, cleanly cut and delicately formed,
nose, lips and chin fine and firm. The eyes were grey, sometimes clear and translucid, sometimes dark, impenetrable,
burning. It was thanks to Racine that night that I saw a little
of what they could express.

What a strange relationship exists between the reader and
his listener. What an extraordinary breaking down of barriers! The listener is suddenly given the freedom of a city
at whose gates he would never have dreamt of knocking. He
may enter forbidden precincts. He may communicate at the
most sacred altars with a soul he has never dared, never will
dare, approach, watch without fear or shame a spirit that has
dropped its arms, its veils, its prudences, its reserves. He who
is not beloved may gaze and hearken and learn at last what
nothing else will ever reveal to him and what he longs to
know even at the cost of life itself—how the beloved face is
moved by passion, how scorn sits upon those features and
anger and love. How the beloved's voice softens and trem-
bles into tenderness or breaks in the anguish of jealousy and
grief. . . . Oh, but it is too soon to say all this! All these are
reflections of a later date.

I have heard many readers read Racine, and famous men
among them, but I have not heard any who read him as well
as Mlle Julie. She read simply and rapidly, without any of
the actor's arts and affectations, with no swelling voice, with
no gestures beyond the occasional lifting of her hand, in which
she held a long ivory paper-cutter. But the gravity of her
bearing and her voice transported me at once into the courts
of princes and the presence of great emotions:

Avant que tous les Grecs vous parlent par ma voix,
Souffrez que j'ose ici me flatter de leur choix,
Et qu'à vos yeux, Seigneur, je montre quelque joie
De voir le fils d'Achille et le vainqueur de Troye . . .

The sonorous vowels, the majestic periods, the tremendous names sweep on; one is borne upon a tide of music and greatness; one follows breathlessly the evolutions, the shiftings, the advances and retreats of the doomed quartet as they tread their measured way to death and madness, through all the vicissitudes of irresolution, passion and jealousy, leaving at the end a child's soul shaken and exhausted, the first great rent made in the veil that hides the emotions of men and women from the eyes of innocence.

Did I understand the play at that first reading? Oh, certainly not. Haven't I put the gathered experience of years into my recollection of it? No doubt. What is certain is that it gave me my first conception of tragedy, of the terror and complication and pity of human lives. Strange that for an English child that revelation should have come through Racine instead of through Shakespeare. But it did.

I went to bed that night in a kind of daze, slept as if I had been drugged and in the morning awoke to a new world—a world of excitement—a world in which everything was fierce and piercing, everything charged with strange emotions, clothed with extraordinary mysteries, and in which I myself seemed to exist only as an inner core of palpitating fire.

The walk that morning, the beauty of the forest, the sky, the deliciousness of the air, the delight of running—for the first time I enjoyed these things consciously.

"I understand," I cried to myself, "I understand at last. Life, life, life, this is life, full to overflowing with every ecstasy and every agony. It is mine, mine to hug, to exhaust, to drain."

And lessons! I went to them with a renovated ardour.
Oh yes, I had been a fairly intelligent pupil; I had enjoyed
learning and working in a kind of humdrum way. This was
something quite different—something I had never known.
Every page of the Latin grammar seemed to hold some passionate secret which must be mine or I should die. Words!
How astonishing they were! The simplest bore with it such
an aura of music and romance as wafted me into fairy-land.
Geography! Oh, to sit poring and wondering over an atlas.
Here were pagodas! There the Nile! Jungles! Deserts!
Coral islands in the Pacific ringed round with lagoons! The
eternal snows of the Himalayas! Aurora Borealis flaming at
the pole! Worlds upon worlds of magic revealed! Why
had I never known of them before? History! Those men!
Those heroes! How they looked, how they smiled as they
were going to the block or the stake! And what had they
died for? Faith, liberty, truth, humanity! What did those
words really represent? I musn't rest till I found out. And
the peoples! The poor sheep-like peoples! Those too must
be thought of. Not yet. I dare not yet. There will be time
enough for that later. I am not strong enough yet to look
really at all those dreadful meaningless pains. I must put that
at the back of my mind. Now, now, I must grow strong. I
must feed on beauty and rapture in order to grow strong.
And first of all that face. There was that to look at. A long
way off, at the end of a table. Passing one on the stairs,
coming suddenly out of a door. Talking to other people.
Listening to other people. And sometimes, rarely, reading
aloud. Had I then never looked at a face before? Why should
the mere sight of it make my heart stand still? What was
there so extraordinarily fascinating in watching it? Was it
more satisfying when it was motionless, when one could im-
print the line of the profile on one's memory, so fine and
grave and austere, the delicate curl of the lip, the almost

imperceptible and indescribably touching, faint hollow of the cheek, the fall of the lashes on the pale skin, the curve of the dark hair on the brow? Or was it when expressions flowed over it so swiftly that one's eyes and one's heart were never quick enough to register them? Laughter was never long absent from it, spreading from the slight quiver of a smile to a ripple, to a tempest of gaiety, passing like a flash of lightning, a flood of colour, transforming, vivifying every feature. So I watched from afar. At meals especially, where I sat some way off but on the opposite side of the table.

There were three tables in the big dining-room; the two heads, at the centre one, sat opposite to each other, as the foreign fashion is, in the middle of each long side. When there were guests or visiting professors, they sat on each side of the ladies. Special dishes were generally served for these honoured ones, and if any remained over, the servant was told to hand it round to the young ladies. Once when this occurred, Mlle Julie cross-examined the girls who had been served in this way:

"Did you like that dish? Honestly now. As much as your English roast beef? No——? Yes——? You don't know? Ah, these English! They have no taste. And you, Olivia, what did you think of it?"

My answer, "Delicious!" was so fervent that she laughed:

"Ha! Have we got a gourmet at last? But appreciation isn't all. There must be discrimination too. Was there anything in the dish that you think might be criticized? Anything that might have improved it?"

"I think——" I murmured——

"Yes, out with it!"

"There was perhaps a thought too much lemon in it."

"Bravo!" she cried. "You deserve encouragement. You shall be promoted."

And at the next meal, after an anxious search, I found my

napkin ring had been placed next to Mlle Julie's own. And it was there, at her right hand, that I sat till the end of my time at Les Avons, unless a visitor or a professor sometimes separated us. And now she almost always helped me herself to one or other of the special dishes, calling me "Mlle Gourmet", asking me my opinion, laughing at my enjoyment, teasing me for being still too "English", because I wouldn't drink wine. "But, perhaps," she said "our *vin ordinaire* isn't good enough for you?" And perhaps, indeed, that was it.

But there was no need of wine to intoxicate me. Everything in her proximity was intoxicating. And I was now, for the first time, within range of her talk. Mlle Julie's talk, I discovered later, was celebrated, and not only amongst us schoolgirls, but amongst famous men, whose names we whispered.

I had no doubt been accustomed, or ought to have been accustomed, to good talk at home. But at home one was inattentive. There were all the other children who somehow interfered. It was on their level, in their turmoil, that one lived. They were too distracting to allow of one's taking any interest in one's elders and their conversation. When one did listen to it, it was mostly political, or else took the form of argument. My mother and my aunt, who was often in the house, had interminable and heated discussions, in which my mother was invariably in the right and my aunt beyond belief inconsequent and passionate. We found them tedious and sometimes nerve-racking. My father, a man, in our eyes, of infinite wisdom and humour, did not talk much; he was fond of explaining scientific or mathematical problems to us, or occasionally, of inventing and making us take a share in some fantastic piece of tomfoolery. He would let fall from time to time a grim and gnomic apophthegm, which we treasured as a household word, and would often calm a heated discussion by an apparently irrelevant absurdity. As for the people who came to the house, many of whom were highly distinguished, we admired them without listening to them. Their world seemed hardly to impinge upon ours.

How different it was here! Mlle Julie was witty. Her brilliant speech darted here and there with the agility and grace of a humming-bird. Sharp and pointed, it would sometimes transfix a victim cruelly. No one was safe, and if one laughed with her, one was liable the next minute to be pierced oneself with a shaft of irony. But she tossed her epigrams about with such evident enjoyment, that if one had the smallest sense of fun, one enjoyed them too, and it was from her that I, for one, learnt to realize the exquisite adaptation of the French tongue to the French wit. But her talk was not all epigrams. One felt it informed by that infectious ardour, that enlivening zest, which were the secret of her success as a schoolmistress. There was nothing into which she could not infuse them. Every subject, however dull it had seemed in the hands of others, became animated in hers. With the traditional culture of a French Protestant family, having contacts with eminent men and women in many countries, she had too a spontaneous and open mind, capable of points of view, fond of the stimulus of paradox. The dullest of her girls was stirred into some sort of life in her presence; to the intelligent, she communicated a Promethean fire which warmed and coloured their whole lives. To sit at table at her right hand was an education in itself.

IV

BUT it must not be supposed that more orthodox studies were neglected or that companionship was wanting. There were four or five of the elder girls who were congenial and friendly. We made a set apart, we were "the clever ones", those who spoke up at the classes, those who attended Mlle Julie's literature lessons and readings, those who were chosen to send in essays to the Paris professors. These essays, or "*devoirs*" as they were called, were the chief torment and excitement of our lives. After the professor's lecture, we had to write out a *résumé* of his discourse, or expand one particular portion of it. We were expected to fill some fifteen or sixteen copy-book pages, had access to a fairly large library, and were supposed to devote the greater part of Thursday and Sunday afternoons to the task in a small study specially reserved for "les grandes". When the *devoir* was finished it was handed on Friday and Monday mornings to Mlle Julie, who looked it over and, if she thought it worthy, passed it on to the professor. It was *her* comments we cared about; the professor was generally, I suppose, a young man fresh from his examinations, cast in a university mould, and very much at sea in talking to this strange collection of "jeunes filles" from barbarous lands. At any rate, we usually had a supreme contempt for him, and, in truth, he was at an overwhelming disadvantage, obliged in spite of himself to endure the ordeal of comparison with an intellect so alive, so widely experienced as Mlle Julie's, with a personality so exceptional, a beauty so striking.

I remember my first *devoir*. It was on Corneille and the "quarrel of the Cid". Do what I would, I could not pad it out to more than six pages. Dry facts, jejune statements were all that I could wring from my subject. I had no notion how to work, how to think, how to co-ordinate. I was desperate.

I remember the night she gave it back to me. Not good enough! It was after dinner. A bevy of us were collected in the long, wide passage, paved with a chequer of black and white marble, which led to the front door, and which we were allowed to use as a kind of promenade deck. It was an evening on which Mlle Julie was going out—to dinner in the town or to an evening party in Paris, somewhere which necessitated evening dress. This was always an occasion, and her devotees would cluster to see her go by in her magnificence and say good-night as she passed. She came sweeping down stairs, Signorina running after her with her fan, her gloves, her handbag. Her evening cloak was thrown back and we could see the shimmer of bare neck and lace and satin.

"*Tiens!*" she said as she caught sight of me. "I was looking for you. Here's your *devoir*. *Un peu pauvre!*" She tossed it to me and swept on.

"Un peu pauvre!" Yes, that was it! That was I! Poor! Poor! It was my first incentive to work, to till my soil, to extract from it all the riches I could, to show—to show her—that, after all, I had some.

Part of the school's programme was that the girls should be taken from time to time to Paris to be shown the sights, the churches, the picture-galleries and so on, and on special occasions to a concert or a play. When Mlle Julie led the party, there were never more than two or three of us and I was always one. Sometimes, greatest treat of all, it would be to a *matinée* at the Français—yes always to the Théâtre Français. In those days it had not been shorn of all its glory. The great tradition was still respected, still intact. Want of faith in its virtues, distrust of its powers, a belief in new standards, new values, new methods, were no doubt already growing outside. They were no doubt already rife on the other bank of the Seine, and Antoine was beginning perhaps to raise his head, but it was only when these dissolvents entered the sacred doors themselves that they proved fatal. In the days of my youth, the prestige of the Comédie Française was still unblown upon. The Sociétaires carried their heads high and there were famous names among them. The consummate art of acting was theirs by divine, by imprescriptible right, and no touch of doubt, or fear of failure, or lack of enthusiasm, or envy of others' success, had insinuated its poison into the great institution.

And so the first time I sat in a *baignoire* with Mlle Julie beside me, and heard the three fateful knocks, and saw the great curtain roll apart, was one of unforgettable, of purest pleasure. It rolled open upon a scene of lovely fancy and romantic cynicism and exquisite elegance. Delaunay was acting one of Musset's heroes, Reichemberg was the *ingénue*, Got the *abbé*, Madeleine Brohan (the survivor of a still more famous past) the old Marquise. Ravishing, ravishing, creatures, whose every word and every movement were wit and grace, and who distilled into one's heart, drop by drop, the delicious satisfaction of perfect finish!

Then there was the *entr'acte*. We walked up and down the long, broad foyer amidst the buzz of animated Parisians; we gazed, at one end, on Voltaire, sitting impish in his armchair, at the other on Molière's weary melancholy; on one long side, the row of big windows looked down on the busy Place below; on the other, were ranged more busts of the Maison's deities—a woman too among them. Then back to the *baignoire*, in a more elevated mood. This time the curtain rolled open on the court of the Caesars; *Britannicus* was the play and Mounet Sully the budding Nero. We watched the growth of evil passions in his face, we heard his voice, more and more raucous, more and more rapid, swell fuller and fuller of lust, hatred and cruelty; when the tempter crept up

[35]

behind him and dropped the insidious poison in his ear, we saw the conflict working in his features, in his almost motionless attitude; we saw the gradual breaking down of virtue's barriers, the increasing rush of oncoming wickedness; we saw the monster still held in respect by Agrippina's lash, we saw him furtive and distraught after his crime,

> ... *ses yeux mal assurés*
> *N'osant lever aux cieux leurs regards égarés*

as he swept hounded from his mother's presence to brood upon her awful prophecy.

On golden days Mlle Julie took me to Paris alone. Golden but exhausting. She would take me by the hand and race me through the galleries at the Louvre, talking torrentially all the time—for pictures seemed to excite her—until we reached the room of her choice. Here she would select a masterpiece for special contemplation and remain silent before it, gazing with fixed intentness. I remember some of those she would so contemplate: Giorgione's *Concert*, Watteau's *Indifférent*, the *Pilgrims of Emmaus*, a Chardin, a Corot. I stood beside her trying to understand. Sometimes she would say, "Now, go and look at *your* favourites." I took this for a dismissal and went off, but my favourite would always be one I could look at without letting her out of the compass of my eye. She would join me after a little, cast a cursory glance at it and say, rather contemptuously, "Pas si mal!" (but she didn't guess the limitations set to my choice).

Then she would begin again to talk, to herself rather than to me: what was the common factor that made each of these pictures a work of art? Could I tell her that? And how with such material substances as canvas, oil, pigments, were such immaterial effects produced? The plastic arts! Had I ever thought how different they were from the other arts, from literature, the art of words? From music, the purest—or was it the impurest—of them all? Had I noticed that Watteau's painting was the painting of a sick man, of a man who had to fly to dreams as a relief from bodily suffering? That his gay celestial visions were the refuge of a man who spat blood? That in the *Voyage to Cythera* there were no bodies but the evanescence of lights and colours? And yet that same art of painting had created *The Pilgrims of Emmaus*. Little atheist that I was, let me learn some divinity, some portion of the meaning of Christianity from the gloom and the radiance of that picture. And so on. Seeds flung at random into the air, some to take root, some, alas, to be lost for ever.

And then she would whirl me off to a fashionable pastry-cook and stuff me with cakes and chocolates, and enjoy her own share too. Afterwards, perhaps, there would be a visit to some of her friends: to an ex-*président du conseil*, whose wife had been one of her pupils (and I was awed to hear him still called Monsieur le Président) or to the widow of a poor professor painfully bringing up three or four children in the Quartier Latin; or to the studio of a famous painter; or to the at-home day of a French Academician. Wherever she flashed, she was welcomed, honoured, spoilt; it was she who became the centre of the talk and the laughter and the cordiality. I sat silent in my corner and wondered at these French, at the readiness of their wits, at their unfailing interest in things of the mind, at the profound seriousness that underlay all this surface brilliance.

When we left the house, Mlle Julie would give me a sketch of the inmates, of some of the tragedies and struggles and successes and failures she had known. She told me of the girl who refused to eat and who was at death's door from starvation, "but I managed to cure her by holding her hand and letting her talk two hours a day . . . it needed a deal of patience." Of the boy who had shot himself, for love, he thought, but really because his poor mother had overworked him. "Ah! that was a dreadful business! There was no curing that grief." Of the despair of a young wife who had lost three children and her husband of diphtheria in one week, and had become the wife of her husband's best friend a few months later. Of the young and beautiful and gifted Margaret X——, recently married to a great savant, who was also a hunchback dwarf. "Poor child! But one has only to look at her eyes to see she's not unhappy. The bride of mysticism!"

On every side of me, strange new worlds were opening. Veil after veil was slowly lifting from life, to leave still further veils and mysteries beyond.

And the background, the setting of such days, was the adorable beauty of Paris. I, who had not yet awakened to the beauty of London, felt that of Paris sink into my very being. Little as I knew of it, little as an English girl could know of it, it seemed to me the quintessence and the symbol of everything I cared for most. The incomparable light in which it was bathed, the river gliding so intimately through its very heart, the noble palaces, the quays, the bridges where one looked alternately west and east, wondering which vista was the more enchanting, the more moving, whether the groves of the Champs Elysées or the towers of Notre Dame—all of this filled me with rapture. And sometimes we drove through the great spaces of the Place de la Concorde, with its giddy stream of life, its fountains and its obelisk, and in one corner the *crêpe*-shrouded figure of Strasbourg. Oh! how those veils smote my heart; there in the midst of all that life and gaiety, stood a monument of grief, a reminder of death and defeat; but one looked away from it, looked further westward and watched the sky turn golden in the distance behind the Arc de Triomphe. The sun was setting indeed, but triumphantly, gloriously, and shedding on the world an ineffable tenderness in its farewell. Then Paris lighted up; one by one, sparkling like fireflies, I thought, the lamps came out in the trees. A minute more and the boulevards were ablaze. A tornado of excitement was whirling round me. Theatres, cafés, music halls! What fever, what intoxication possessed those crowds? I should have liked to know, I should have liked to rush with them to their pleasures, to drink their draughts of life and exhilaration. But no; not yet. I was only a girl, and besides, it was time to go home. There was more than an hour's train journey and we shouldn't be back till late.

The train was generally empty at that time. Mlle Julie would lean back in a corner of the dimly lighted carriage and I liked to sit opposite and look at her. I could often do so for a long time without indiscretion, for her eyes were shut. No, she wasn't asleep, but tired. I watched the eyelashes on the cheek, the soft resting eyelids. Was it tired she looked? Not so much tired as sad. Not so much sad as serious. No, it wasn't bitterness in the curving corner of her lips, but an extraordinary sweetness, an extraordinary gravity, an extraordinary nobility. What were her thoughts? Behind those closed lids, what was going on? What had her life been? Had she suffered? She must have suffered to look so grave. Had she loved? Whom had she loved? I think the passion that devoured me at that time was the passion of curiosity. Once, as I was watching her like this, she suddenly opened her eyes and caught me. Her glance held me for a moment, and I was too fascinated to look away. Her glance was piercing, not unkind but terrifying. She was searching me. What did she see?

"Come," she said at last. "Come here and sit beside me." I think she said it to get rid of my intolerable gaze. After I had obeyed, she put her hand on mine for the space of a heartbeat. I turned my eager palm to clasp it, but she withdrew it gently and sank back again into her corner and her reverie.

[39]

V

IT was not till I was well on in my first term, with all its novelties and distractions, that I became aware that there was an uneasiness in the atmosphere.

I have said very little so far of Mlle Cara, but she too was a pervading influence—the influence of an invalid. "Oh," the girls said at first, "she isn't strong enough to do much in the school. She just takes the little ones." But that was not every day: only on the days she felt well. On those days, the time-table was recklessly disregarded and everything had to give way—lessons, walks, practising, no matter what, went by the board. When the cry went up, "Les petites pour Mlle Cara!" there was a stampede and off they rushed. She had her own methods of flattering, cajoling and amusing them. But, I gathered, everyone was not so pleased. This irregularity was upsetting. Classes were disturbed. Mistresses who were off duty had to remain at hand, liable to be called upon at any moment, for it was not unusual for the little ones' French hour to end as abruptly as it had begun. They would steal out of her room with anxious faces. "The migraine!" they whispered. And sometimes, "She cried again to-day." On those days, Mlle Cara would not appear at meals and Mlle Julie, visibly anxious, would speak sharply or not at all, would hurry over dessert and give the signal for dismissing us almost before we had finished our last mouthful.

"What is the matter with Mlle Cara?" I asked Signorina.

"Nobody knows. For my part, I think nothing. When she chooses she's as well as anybody. Last holidays she didn't have a single migraine. There was nothing she wasn't up to —plays, concerts, walks. She was up and out all the time."

"Perhaps she overdid it."

"Perhaps. The very day Mlle Julie came back, so did the migraines."

"Does she have the doctor?"

"Sometimes. He doesn't seem to prescribe anything very definite. Sometimes a sleeping-draught. Mlle Julie always says, 'He tells me it's nothing.' But it worries her dreadfully all the same. For my part——"

"What, for your part?"

"She does it on purpose."

"On purpose for what?"

"To worry her. And then——"

"And then?"

"Frau Riesener——"

"Yes?"

"Encourages her."

"Why?"

"I know why——. But we've talked enough now. You must say your sonnet."

And I began:

> *Tanto gentile e tanto onesta pare*
> *La donna mia quand'ella altrui saluta*
> *Ch'ogni lingua divien tremando, muta,*
> *E gli occhi non l'ardiscon di guardare.*

It was easy to learn that.

Whatever might be the reason, it was plain enough that Frau Riesener and Signorina detested each other. They were more or less the heads of rival factions—"the Cara-ites" and the "Julie-ites". Yes, that was it. The "Julie-ites" gravitated to Signorina and learnt Italian, the "Cara-ites" to Frau Riesener and learnt German.

"I've won my bet," said Nina one morning to Mimi. "It was a bet about you, Olivia."

"Oh, how exciting!"

"I'm sorry I've lost," said Mimi.

"Yes, the first minute I set eyes on you, I knew you'd be a Julie-ite. I gave her a week, didn't I, Mimi?"

"Yes," answered Mimi gloomily. "You've won."

So I was a Julie-ite. I didn't much care for the appellation. But it was true that it hadn't taken me a week to make up my mind about our two heads. And yet Mlle Cara was extraordinarily kind. She would often invite me with Mimi and one or two others to have coffee in her *cabinet de travail*. She would call me by caressing names, she would talk to me about my dear Mamma and my little brothers and sisters, she would tell me she had heard I was so clever, and I must be an honour to the school. She would admire my clothes. She was all softness and sweetness, but she made me feel uncomfortable. After a time I dreaded the visits to the *cabinet de travail*. Mlle Cara's coaxings and wheedlings got on my nerves. One day she looked at me reproachfully and said:

"You don't like me, *ma petite*. Why is that? Haven't I been kind to you?"

"Oh, Mademoiselle," I cried, horrified, "of course you have. Very, very kind. I'm truly grateful."

"Go away!" she said brusquely. "Go down to the library, since that's what you prefer."

And then I knew it was true. I didn't like her. Better, oh, much better than Mlle Cara's *cabinet de travail* I liked the library, though there I was not flattered or coaxed, sometimes treated roughly, sometimes ignored, and sometimes again carried up into sublime heights of enthusiasm, excitement, rapture.

VI

I SPENT three terms at Les Avons, but cannot divide the growth of my experience into terms, nor always remember with exactness the order of the events which were important in my story. For instance, when was it that Laura came to stay? After the summer or after the Christmas holidays? But the holidays did not count for me. They were mere tracts of time to be got through—pauses, in which, no doubt, 1 continued to grow, to develop, to become formed in body and mind, but unconsciously. I seemed to myself not to be really alive during the holidays, to be somebody acting a part and pretending to be present, pretending to be myself, while all the while the real I was somewhere else.

Not that I was unhappy during that first period, either at home or at school. There was gaiety, there were talks, there were friends. And I was never conscious of any jealousy or envy or dislike from companions who could not but see that I was favoured. The common herd, as I contemptuously called them in my thoughts, were incapable of feeling envy of the privileges which I enjoyed, and which they did not want and very likely did not notice. But the others—my friends and equals—they, who might have envied me, seemed to think that all I received was my due. Not that *they* did not appreciate Mlle Julie's favours, oh yes, they knew their price, but allowed me, I don't know why, an undisputed right to enjoy them.

Dear, mild, scrupulous Gertrude, taken from a commonplace, middle-class English family and suddenly dumped into this hot-bed of foreign culture, suddenly subjected to the stimulus of Mlle Julie's personality, how anxious she was to profit, to learn, to acquire knowledge and grace! How she grew to realize the unbridgeable chasm between the life to which she belonged by birth and circumstance and this world of which Mlle Julie held the keys! How she grew to fear that all her efforts would be vain, that she had been uprooted, not transplanted, and that she would never find a soil in which to thrive! How then she pined and wilted to a tragic end!

Edith, my friend, who loved me better than I loved her, who had all the qualities that I lacked, who had a clearer, cooler, saner brain, but who could yet endure, and even admire, my fits of humour, my enthusiasms, my excitements, without reproving them and without sharing them.

Georgie, strange dark-eyed Georgie! There was nothing intellectual about *her*. But I guessed she had already lived with greater intensity than any of us. She hid some mysterious ardour in her own breast, near which mine too gathered heat.

Turbulent, undisciplined, Irish Nina, for ever in and out of scrapes, so concerned when she was in, so reckless when she was out, so generous, so warm-hearted, so amusing in her outbreaks of rebellion, that even authority smiled in checking them—how fond I was of her—and of Mimi too. Mimi, the will-o'-the-wisp, incapable of learning anything out of a book and skilful at a hundred other things; who could toss up a fancy-dress in half an hour, and arrange a bunch of flowers, and sing like an angel, and mimic like a monkey. Her company delighted me, though my graver friends wondered why.

There were others, of course, whom I didn't like, whom I thought mean, dull, affected, irritating. But I didn't frequent them. Why should I? We let each other be. I had enough to fill my heart and mind without them.

But it is of Laura I must speak now. I had looked forward to her coming, I confess, with a good deal of apprehension. "Mlle Julie's favourite—the most favourite favourite she has ever had," said some of the older girls, who had been new during Laura's last term. They spoke with admiration and almost with awe of her "cleverness", that schoolgirl word for every kind of excellence at "lessons". Her *devoirs* were always the best; they used to be read aloud as examples of what a *devoir* might be, ought to be. When she went up to the blackboard to do a problem in algebra or geometry, the professor used to say, "Je vous félicite, Mademoiselle". She read *Faust* with Frau Riesener and the *Divina Commedia* with Signorina. Did Signorina like her, I asked. As for me, I knew I should hate her.

"Oh no," said Signorina, "I don't think you will."

"But she's altogether too perfect. How can one like such a paragon? And besides, she'll despise me. And never speak to me. And besides she'll always be in the library, and——"

"In fact," said Signorina, "you've made up your mind to be jealous, Olivia mia. I strongly advise you to get over that little failing, or else——" her voice dropped, did it tremble? "——you're in for a bad time."

But the first time I saw Laura, I felt nothing of what I had expected to feel, of what I had determined to feel. I was conquered afresh as I had been by the first sight of her photograph. No, it was impossible to be jealous of Laura.

When Mlle Julie called me into the library and introduced us to each other, we were both shy and awkward, but Laura more awkward than I, and I soon realized that, instead of feeling herself superior, on the contrary, she was curiously conscious of her deficiencies. She knew that, in spite of her efforts, she was badly dressed and clumsy, that she had neither beauty, nor grace, nor manner, nothing, in fact, to atone for her intellectual superiority, while at the same time she had an uneasy feeling that that superiority ought somehow to be atoned for. Not that this want of confidence in her powers of attraction made her self-conscious. No, I have never seen anyone freer from every sort of selfishness, never seen anyone devote herself to others with such manifest gladness. And yet, with all her altruism, one could never think of her as self-sacrificing. She never did sacrifice herself. She had no self to sacrifice. When she gave her time, her thoughts, her energies to bringing up her stepbrothers and stepsisters, it was *really* a joy to her. When her father married again and she lost her position as mistress of his household—a great position, for he was perhaps the most important man in England at the time—she welcomed her young stepmother with such a warmth of affection, of sympathy, of gratitude to her for bringing happiness to the father she loved, that no one could pity her; one felt she was *really* glad. Her face was one of the most radiant I have ever seen; grave sometimes, but never moody, never despondent. Her clear, untroubled eyes looked at one with such frank, joyful affection that for the moment she banished moodiness and despondency from oneself too.

She was an invigorating companion. We talked of many things. Not so much of politics at that time, for I was too remote from that world to take an intelligent interest in it, but of character, of ambitions, of morals, of conduct, and of certain elementary notions of metaphysics which I was beginning to read a little; very rarely of persons. It was while we were walking up and down the long black-and-white-paved passage that we talked; but we often sat in the library too, for far from trying to keep me out of the library, far from wanting to be there alone with Mlle Julie, it was Laura who always came to fetch me when there was a chance; it was she who made me familiar with it, so that even after she had left, I often used to go there uninvited.

In the library, we listened to Mlle Julie's reading. This was desultory enough and often interrupted by conversation, in which my part was that of a listener. Sometimes it would be an article from a review that she read us, on a living author or a Renaissance painter, sometimes a chapter of a book—a page of Michelet's or Renan's—sometimes a poem—a Victor Hugo or a Vigny. Sometimes it was one of us who had to read to her. Often she would make us look up a reference in the big Larousse, sometimes she would show us her collection of photographs, of which she had large stocks gathered on her travels. It was generally the spare hour after lunch and dinner that we spent with her in this way, and generally when we left her Signorina would come in to help her with the day's correspondence and accounts.

"Laura," I said to her one day towards the end of her stay, "do you love her?"

"Oh," said Laura, "you know I do. She has been the best part of my life. My father's too busy to talk to me much. She has opened my eyes to all I like best in the world, showered me with innumerable treasures."

"And tell me this, Laura. Does your heart beat when you go into the room where she is? Does it stand still when you touch her hand? Does your voice dry up in your throat when you speak to her? Do you hardly dare raise your eyes to look at her, and yet not succeed in turning them away?"

"No," said Laura. "None of all that."

"What then?" I insisted.

"Why," said Laura, looking at me with her clear, untroubled eyes, which had a kind of wonder and a kind of recoil in them: "there's nothing else. I just love her."

"So," thought I to myself, but I didn't say it aloud, "my feeling is not just love. Is it something more or something less? My heart is not as great as Laura's, but I won't admit that it feels less. Surely, surely, it feels more—but perhaps not more, perhaps only differently."

Laura's visit came to an end unexpectedly soon. She had a letter from home calling her back. But to me she said privately:

"I think Mlle Cara is unwell. Or perhaps I tire or irritate her. I feel it's better for Mlle Julie that I should go."

"Oh, Laura," I cried, "when shall I see you again?"

"When you leave school, we shall see each other very often. We're going to be friends all our lives."

And so, dear Laura, we have been.

No, it was not Laura I was jealous of; it was rather, for some inexplicable reason, of Cécile. Cécile was our American beauty. Tall, elegant, exquisitely dressed, with a lovely little head as perfectly finished as a Tanagra's, a dazzling skin of cream and roses, and dark, lively, empty eyes. Why was I jealous of Cécile? She had, I thought, neither heart nor brains. She went on her way with a kind of impervious, serene, good-tempered aloofness. One felt she was absolutely secure in her own superiority. Mlle Julie was very fond of talking to her and trying to tease her. She used to admire her clothes, criticize her style of hair-dressing, constantly make remarks about her personal appearance.

"Personal remarks!" she exclaimed once. "I know you English have a horror of them. You're brought up to avoid them. It's ill-bred, you think, to say to someone, 'Your hair's beautiful, but you dress it unbecomingly.' In fact, it's indiscreet, an intrusion, almost an outrage to think at all about the person you are talking to—just as you must pretend never to notice what you're eating. To my mind, the making of personal remarks is one of the most important things in life. How can one live without remarking other people, and accustoming oneself to remark them justly? And if some of one's remarks come to one's lips, it just gives salt and savour to one's conversation. You'd rather I talked to you about your clothes and your hair than about the works of Pascal, wouldn't you, Cécile?"

"Oh yes, much," said Cécile—though she hadn't the least idea who Pascal was.

"Well, I'll tell you what I think. I daresay you know more about it than I do, but I'll give you my opinion for what it's worth. You're beautiful enough to justify your giving your whole time to the care of your beauty. But you must try, if possible, to do it intelligently. When you marry your duke—you do mean to marry an English duke, don't you?"

"Yes," said Cécile, with calm conviction. (And she did.)

"Well, when you marry him, remember that though fashion is important, you are beautiful enough not to be the slave of fashion. Some of your countrywomen are so admirably turned out, so extraordinarily 'shop-finished' that they lose all their charm. Try to be perfect without showing it too much. Or rather, remember you are so perfect that you needn't bother too much about showing it.—Is there anyone else here who would like to marry a duke?" she went on, looking round.

"I should," said I, "very much."

"Ah," said Mlle Julie, examining me critically, "I'm not surprised. But, chère petite, I'm afraid you never will. Haven't you a second choice?"

"Yes," I said, "the duke's my second choice. I'd rather marry (I didn't dare say 'be loved by' but that's what I meant) a great man—a poet, an artist. But I shall never do that either."

"I'm not so sure of that," she answered gravely.

And yet, though I knew I was respected more than Cécile, there were moments when I envied her for her beauty, for her finish, for that immense power she had, without any effort, of making herself felt, moments when it wasn't respect I wanted but something more—human, I called it.

I was envious too in a different way of Signorina. I was conscious of a singleness in her passion of which I knew I was incapable. There was nothing in her which she had not devoted to her idol. Yes, I knew that with her, passion had obliterated every other feeling—jealousy even had been burnt up in the white heat of her adoration. I guessed that scruples, conscience, all idea of other duties, all other interests, engagements, affections, save as they related to this particular devotion, no longer existed for her. This gave her an extraordinary calm. There was nothing whatever conflicting in her. She was never traversed by those tempests of despair and resentment with their concomitant fits of self-contempt and self-loathing which so often shook me. I think she wanted nothing for herself but to be allowed to serve—to serve in any way—in every way. I think there was nothing else she wanted. If I too would have liked to serve, I was continually conscious that I was incapable and unworthy, continually devoured by vain humilities. And then there was also in me a curious repugnance, a terror of getting *too* near. I should not have liked to help Mlle Julie at her toilette, to brush her hair, to put on her shoes for her. When I thought of the particular services which Signorina performed with such entire gladness, I found myself shuddering. And then too, what about those other things that inhabited me? Wasn't I likely to be caught up into excitement by a thousand extraneous causes? A curve of the river between its wooded banks, a mass of clouds in the sky, a line of poetry, a scene in a novel, the rapture of seeing the curtain roll back at the theatre, anguish for Swift's madness, for Keats' death—these were a few of my countless infidelities. I defended myself at the bar of my private tribunal by saying that all these emotions were but "the ministers of love" and that Love himself had created them "to feed his sacred flame." But nevertheless I sometimes envied and very often admired Signorina.

VII

I REMEMBER the first éclat I witnessed between the ladies. For some weeks there had been whisperings among the girls that they were falling out; raised voices, angry words had been heard by people who passed by their door. But the first public scene took place at table. It was typical of all the others and started from a trifle.

Hortense, the maid-servant, dropped a plate behind Mlle Cara's chair, and Mlle Cara gave a start and a scream as if she had been shot.

"The girl did it on purpose. I know she did," she exclaimed.

"Oh, Cara, I'm so sorry she startled you," said Mlle Julie.

"No, you're not," shrieked Mlle Cara. "You're laughing at me. And you encourage her clumsiness. It was you and Mlle Baietto who engaged her. You knew she was totally unsuitable. But of course, you never listen to me."

Mlle Julie tried to turn the attack.

"Well, in the meantime, we'll get her to wait at the other table."

Another time Mlle Cara complained of the food. She pushed away her plate impatiently.

"No one ever pays the faintest attention to my régime," she cried. "And yet I should have thought Mlle Baietto knew by this time that I can't eat beef. I believe you're all trying to poison me."

"But, Cara," said Mlle Julie, "here's your chicken just been put on the table."

"It's too late. I can't eat anything now." She got up to leave the table. Mlle Julie rose too and made a movement to accompany her, but Frau Riesener was beforehand with her.

She hurried up to give Mlle Cara a supporting arm, and as they walked slowly from the room, Mlle Julie dropped back into her chair.

My lesson with Signorina that afternoon was an agitated one.

"Oh," she cried, "Heaven knows I do my very best to give her food she'll like. But it's no use. She's determined to find fault with everything."

"Why does she hate you?"

"Oh, it's not me she hates, or only in the second place. What she wants is to torture *her*. It's bad enough now at table, but upstairs she's getting more and more uncontrolled. She sobs and cries. She says she's dying, that we're all killing her. I listened at the door the other day. It was dreadful. 'You don't love me,' she kept repeating; 'nobody loves me.' And then I heard Mlle Julie answer so tenderly, so sweetly, 'Yes, Cara, indeed I do. I long for you to be well and happy.' And Mlle Cara went on again. I made it out through her sobs: 'No, no. You take everyone's affection away from me. First one and then the other. They begin by liking me and then they change. You steal them from me.' And then, Olivia, I heard your name. 'I thought Olivia would like me, but it's you she likes, always you.'"

"It's not my fault," I cried. "How can I help it?"

It was during my Italian lessons (and it may be believed that I learnt to understand and speak that language with uncommon facility) that I managed to piece together odds and ends of facts over which my imagination first brooded and then built its fantasies. But how far they were really facts, or Signorina's coloured version of them, I never knew. And from first to last of this obscure history, I was nearly always at the outside edge of it, trying to grope my way into its heart, trying with my inexperience of all the fundamental elements of human nature, and my ignorance of most of the actual circumstances, to understand what was going on, to figure to myself the feelings and motives of the actors in it. Of course I never succeeded. And even now . . . no, even now I am still in the same uncertainty. Clouds of suspicion and surmise gather and form round first one and then the other of the characters in the drama, but clouds so unsubstantial and so vague that they dissolve at a breath and shape themselves in other forms and other colours, that they often seem to me to be the unwholesome exhalations of my own disordered heart and mind.

Mlle Julie, then, and Mlle Cara (so Signorina told me) had lived together for about fifteen years. They were both young, beautiful and gifted when they first met and decided to become partners in starting a girls' school. It was Julie who had the capital, the influential friends, the energy, the intellect, the commanding personality. It was Cara who had the charm that gained fond mothers' hearts and the qualifications that made the enterprise possible. She had passed all the necessary examinations, and Julie none. They had begun in a small way, but had soon become surprisingly successful, increased their numbers, widened their circle, moved into a larger house, built a library and a music-room. They were something of an institution among a certain set of Parisian intellectuals. Julie was the daughter of a well-known man of letters; her father's friends had been distinguished and at his death had continued their friendship for his brilliant daughter. Julie was eminently sociable and Cara's caressing, cooing manners softened her abruptness and sweetened her epigrams; together they made their drawing-room an attractive place with the added charm of the jeunes filles who flitted in and out of it, ministering cakes and coffee to the guests. They were a model couple, deeply attached, tenderly devoted, the gifts of each supplementing the deficiencies of the other. They were admired and loved. They were happy.

According to Signorina, this harmony had lasted undisturbed until the arrival of Frau Riesener three years ago. Signorina herself had come to the school a month or two earlier. At the beginning, being extremely young, she had filled a very subordinate position.

"Nobody thought anything of me then," she said, "but I have eyes and I watched." (Signorina's eyes were indeed surprisingly bright. She reminded me of a little mouse, whisking along with such astonishing rapidity, appearing and disappearing so unexpectedly, picking up crumbs of information with such deftness.)

Frau Riesener had started by making herself agreeable and almost indispensable to both the ladies. A very capable, very intelligent woman, she had introduced new methods of organization, was informed of the latest theories of education, was extremely clever at finding good teachers, and spared no pains to do so efficiently. Mlle Julie had more time to devote to her special classes of literature and history, more time for visiting her friends in Paris. Mlle Cara was relieved of many household cares and not allowed to fatigue herself, as Frau Riesener said, uselessly.

"But I noticed," said Signorina, "that these attentions had the effect—I don't know whether they had the intention—of separating the friends."

Mlle Cara was always being asked whether she hadn't a headache, always being told she looked tired, always being urged to lie down. Mlle Julie's library was jealously guarded from intrusion. She must not be disturbed at her work. Her visits to Paris were facilitated and encouraged. The breath of outside air was what gave the school its *cachet*, said Frau Riesener; it would be absurd to let them be interfered with by less important duties, which could be as well discharged by a subordinate—by herself, in fact.

And so, from being a prop on which both the friends

leaned, each on her different side, she turned gradually into a barrier between them.

"And then," said Signorina, "her methods changed." As Mlle Julie was often away or often absorbed in her particular tasks, Frau Riesener established her hold more and more completely on Mlle Cara—a hold, which from being enveloping turned dominating, while Mlle Cara became more attached, more clinging, more subservient. She gradually sank—she was actually encouraged to sink—into invalidism. Every ailment was made the most of, every healthy reaction nipped in the bud, and the campaign of insinuation was begun. She was artfully led to believe that Mlle Julie didn't understand her case, that, so strong herself, she was unsympathetic, indifferent to the sufferings of others, that she cared only for her own amusement and neglected her friend and her school. Often, Signorina said, she had heard conversations like the following:

"Come into the garden, Cara."

"Do you think you'd better, Mlle Cara?" Frau Riesener would say. "It's very wet underfoot."

"Would you like me to read to you to-night, Cara?"

"Oh, Mlle Julie, Mlle Cara has had such a tiring day. I'm afraid it might make her head worse."

"Won't you come to the R——'s to-morrow, Cara? They've asked us to lunch."

"Oh Julie, you know I can't. It's far too exhausting. And really, if Minnie R—— had wanted me, I think she might have written to *me*. Don't you think so too, Frau Riesener?"

When was the motive of jealousy introduced? When did it become all-important? Obviously, as Mlle Cara was more and more withdrawn from her friend's companionship, the latter's vitality sought other outlets. Signorina herself crept gradually, unobtrusively into her affections. Frau Riesener had been glad enough at first to make use of her.

"I was so small," repeated Signorina, "that nobody noticed me—except Mlle Julie. She recognized me from the first day. She knew at once what I was capable of. Oh, how good she was to me, Olivia mia! When she found me first, we were starving in Paris, my mother, my sister and I. She took infinite pains to help us—provided hospitals, doctors, nurses, for my mother; established my sister as an Italian teacher in half a dozen wealthy families; and made *me* come to help her here. And so I do," Signorina added, "and so I will, till the end of life."

"For that matter," she went on, "why should Mlle Cara be more jealous of me than Mlle Julie of Frau Riesener?" In any case, the breach had widened, deepened. No smallest incident now but was distorted into a grievance. Complaints had become reproaches, reproaches were turning into taunts.

"How long can it last? What will be the end? And I assure you, Olivia, Mlle Julie bears it all with extraordinary patience. I have never known her return an angry answer. She does all she can to soothe and pacify; she gives her the most devoted attention—when she is allowed to. She does everything, everything except——"

"Except?"

"Except give up her friends. Give up those who love her—those she loves. 'What should I have left?' she said to me once, 'if I were to let you go?' And she told me that Mlle Cara and Frau Riesener were making a concerted attempt to get rid of me. 'Will it be too painful for you, I wonder, *mon enfant*, to stay on, with them against you?' she asked me once. But there was no need for me to answer. And then everything got worse when Laura came. And if Laura hadn't been a saint—a sublime, unconscious saint—I don't know what would have happened. But I believe Laura, without the smallest hypocrisy, was devoted too to Mlle Cara. I think

Mlle Cara was able to believe that she had her affection and that Mlle Julie only cared for her because of her intelligence. This time, however, Laura understood. She was right to cut her visit short, though it won't do much good—for now—" a pause, a sombre pause—"for now, there's you."

Let me think of those words later, I said to myself, there's too much in them—too much joy and terror. I must brush them aside for the moment. I must keep them, bury them, like a dog his bone, till I can return to them alone.

"But what is Frau Riesener's object?" I asked. "Why does she want to separate them? Is it just pure love of mischief-making?"

"I believe," said Signorina slowly and reflectively, "I believe it was so at first, or love of power rather than of mischief. But now I think what she really wants is to drive Mlle Julie away and step into her shoes."

Something incomprehensible it was that Signorina had said: that Mlle Julie had only cared for Laura's intelligence. But hadn't I seen with my own eyes their affection manifested in fifty different ways, the obvious ease and happiness of their relationship? But Mlle Cara had not been jealous of Laura, neither was I jealous of her. "But now there's you," Signorina had said. So there was something different about me. Was it simply that I wasn't a sublime, unconscious saint? That I wasn't generous enough to be fond of Mlle Cara. Something perhaps different from that lay at the back of her remark. Nobody could say that Mlle Julie cared for my intellect. Oh, my intellect couldn't compare with Laura's. I had none of her gifts, I was totally unable to carry on a conversation with Mlle Julie on a footing of equality. Then why should Mlle Cara mind about me? Why should Signorina have said so sombrely, "And now there's you?" So they must think she cares for me more than for Laura. Insensate thought! No, no, not more. But she cares a little.

And differently. Just as I cared for her differently. And now I understood that it was that difference I wanted.

But Laura had been a saint. It was because of that that the breach between the two friends had not become a catastrophe. But I—I was not a saint. How could I be one? And so perhaps it was I who was going to bring that catastrophe about. I couldn't help it. If it depended on altering the feelings in my heart, I was no more capable of doing that than of plucking the heart out of my breast—and I didn't want to. On the contrary. A strange exaltation filled me. Oh no, I wasn't a saint.

Why had Signorina told me all this story? Because I wanted to hear it so? Wasn't it as a warning, too? A warning then, given in vain, for there was nothing I could alter, nothing I would try to alter.

And then my thoughts went back to that past when they had been both young, both beautiful, both happy. Like a wedded couple, I thought. And when couples who have loved part, what a tragedy is that! What disillusionment, what self-reproach, what regrets were eating my beloved's heart out. It was that that had hollowed her cheek, that had made the sensitive curve of her lips so sad, so bitter. And I could do nothing for her. Yet oh! I sighed, how willingly I would die to make her happy.

It was not long after this talk with Signorina, and a day or two after Laura had left, that I gathered up my courage and went by myself to the library at the usual hour. I stood for a minute or two outside the door before turning the handle. When I was alone, I always stood so before the door which was shut between her and me. It seemed an almost super-human effort to open it. It wasn't exactly fear that stopped me. No, but a kind of religious awe. The next step was too grave, too portentous to be taken without preparation—the step which was to abolish absence. All one's fortitude, all one's powers, must be summoned and concentrated to enable one to endure that overwhelming change. She is behind that door. The door will open and I shall be in her presence.

"Is that you, Olivia? Come in."

"May I?"

"Yes. I was feeling lonely without Laura. I'm glad you've come. But I'm busy. You needn't go though. Take a book and read. The Sainte-Beuves are over there. You'd better take a *Lundi*."

"May I take a poet?"

"Yes, certainly. What do you want?"

"The Vigny you were reading yesterday."

'Yes. There it is."

I took the little red volume and sat down on the floor.

How happy I was!

I could see her sitting at her table. I could see her beautiful, serious profile, when I raised my eyes from my book, and when I dropped them I could still feel she was there.

I re-read the *Moïse*.

Greatness and loneliness. "Puissant et solitaire." To live above the crowd in loneliness. To be condemned to loneliness by the greatness of one's qualities. To be condemned to live apart, however much one wanted the contact of warm human companionship. To be the Lord's anointed! Strange and dreadful fate! I forgot where I was as I thought of it. At last I raised my head and saw her eyes fixed upon me. Without knowing what I was doing, without reflection, as if moved by some independent spring of whose existence I was unaware, and whose violence I was totally unable to resist, I suddenly found myself kneeling before her, kissing her hands, crying out over and over again, "I love you!"—sobbing, "I love you!"

Can I remember what she said, what she did? No. Nothing. I can only remember myself kneeling beside her—the feel of her woollen dress on my cheeks, the feel of her hands, the softness and warmth of her hands under my lips, the hardness of her rings. I don't know how I left the room. The rest of the day I lived in a kind of maze, dreaming of those hands, of those kisses.

VIII

IT was at this time that a change came over me. That delicious sensation of gladness, of lightness, of springing vitality, that consciousness of youth and strength and ardour, that feeling that some divine power had suddenly granted me an undreamt-of felicity and made me free of boundless kingdoms and untold wealth, faded as mysteriously as it had come and was succeeded by a very different state. Now I was all moroseness and gloom—heavy-hearted, leaden-footed. I could take no interest in my lessons; it was impossible to think of them. When, on Thursdays and Sundays, I sat with the other girls in our study where we were supposed to be writing our *devoirs*, I could not work. I sat for hours, my arms folded on the table in front of me, my head resting on them, plunged in a kind of coma.

"What on earth are you doing, Olivia?" a friend would ask. "Are you asleep?"

"Oh, leave me alone," I would cry impatiently. "I'm thinking."

But I wasn't thinking. I was sometimes dreaming—the foolish dreams of adolescence: of how I should save her life at the cost of my own by some heroic deed, of how she would kiss me on my death-bed, of how I should kneel at hers and what her dying word would be, of how I should become famous by writing poems which no one would know were inspired by her, of how one day she would guess it, and so on and so on.

At other times I wasn't even dreaming, but just a mass of physical sensations which bewildered me, which made me feel positively sick. My heart beat violently, my breath came fast and unevenly, with the expectation of some extraordinary event which was going to happen the very next minute. At the opening of every door, at the sound of the most casual footstep, my solar plexus shot the wildest stabs through every portion of my body, and the next minute, when nothing had happened, I collapsed, a pricked bladder, into flat and dreary quiescence. Sometimes I was possessed by longing, but I didn't know for what—for some vague blessing, some unimaginable satisfaction, which seemed to be tantalizingly near but which, all the same, I knew was unattainable—a blessing, which, if I could only grasp it, would quench my thirst, still my pulses, give me an Elysian peace. At other times, it was the power of expression that seemed maddeningly denied me. If only I could express myself—in words, in music, anyhow. I imagined myself a *prima donna* or a great actress. Oh, heavenly relief! Oh, an outlet for all this ferment which was boiling within me! Perilous stuff! If I could only get rid of it—shout it to the world—declaim it away!

Then there was a more passive, a more languorous state, when I seemed to myself dissolving, when I let myself go, as I phrased it to myself, when I felt as though I were floating luxuriously down a warm, gentle river, every muscle relaxed, every portion of me open to receive each softest caress of air and water, down, down, towards some unknown, delicious sea. My indefinite desire was like some pervading, unlocalized ache of my whole being. If I could only know, thought I, where it lies, what it is. In my heart? In my brain? In my body? But no, all I felt was that I desired something. Sometimes I thought it was to be loved in return. But that seemed to me so entirely impossible that it was really and truly unimaginable. I could not imagine *how* she could love me. *Like* me, be fond of me, as a child, as a pupil, yes, of course. But that had nothing to do with what I felt. And so I made myself another dream. It was a man I loved as I loved her, and then he would take me in his arms . . . and kiss me . . . I should feel his lips on my cheeks, on my eyelids, on my—— No, no, no, that way lay madness. All this was different— hopeless. Hopeless! A dreadful word, but with a kind of tonic in it. I would hug it to my heart. Yes, hopeless. It was that that gave my passion dignity, that made it worthy of respect. No other love, no love of man and woman could ever be as disinterested as mine. It was I alone who loved— it was I alone whose love was an impossible fantasy.

And yet she sometimes showered me with marvellous kind- nesses. Often when she was reading aloud to me in the library, she would drop her hand into mine and let me hold it. Once when I had a cold, she visited me in my room, petted me, brought me delicacies from the table, told me stories that made me laugh, left me cheerful and contented. It was dur- ing my convalescence from that little indisposition that she put her head into my room one evening and said:

"I'm going out to dinner in Paris, but I'll look in on you when I get back and see how you are and say good-night to you." Her good-night was gay and tender and the next day I was well.

A fortnight later she went out to dinner again. The last train from Paris reached the station at about half-past eleven and she used to be up at the house a little before twelve. How could I help keeping awake that night, half expecting her, listening for her? She had to pass my door to go to her room. Perhaps, perhaps she would come in again. Ah, straining ears and beating heart! But why was she so long? What could she be doing? Again and again I lit my candle and looked at my watch. Can she have passed the door without my having heard her? Impossible! At last, at last, the step came sounding down the long passage. Nearer, nearer. Would it stop? Would it go on? It stopped. A breathless pause. Would the handle turn? It turned. She came in in the dim light of the unshuttered room and stood beside my bed:

"I've brought you a sweet, you greedy little thing," she said and pulled it out of her bag.

Oh yes, I was greedy, but not for sweets. Her hands were my possession. I covered them with kisses.

"There, there, Olivia," she said. "You're too passionate, my child."

Her lips brushed my forehead and she was gone.

It was a little later that we had the usual Mardi Gras fancy-dress ball. Oh, yes, it was exactly like all other girls' school fancy-dress balls. There was a day's disorganization, while the dresses were being made and we were allowed to run about as we would into each other's rooms, chattering, laughing, trying on, madly sewing and pinning. And then came the excitement of the evening. The two ladies sat enthroned with the staff at one end of the music-room, which had been cleared for dancing; a march was played on the piano and we filed past them two and two, made our bows and our curtsies, were questioned, complimented and laughed at. Mlle Julie was in her element on such occasions. To-night was no exception. There was something happier in the atmosphere, a relaxation of tension. Mlle Cara was smiling and cheerful; Mlle Julie's wit sparkled like her eyes; she was enjoying it all as much as anyone. We could see her curiosity, her interest in the different self that each girl revealed in her disguise, some betraying their secret longings and fantasies, some abandoning themselves recklessly to their own natural propensities.

So, it was Mary Queen of Scots that poor, plain Gertrude so pathetically aspired to be; Georgie's dark eyes burned mysterious and tragic beneath a top hat; with her false moustache and pointed beard, she made a marvellous romantic poet of 1830. On her arm hung Mimi, a charming little grisette in a poke bonnet, a shawl and a crinoline, and the two flirted outrageously to every one's delight. Madcap Nina was Puck himself, a torment and an amusement to the whole company. And I? I don't know what my dress revealed. It was a Parsee lady's dress which my mother had brought home from India. Very rich and splendid, I thought. The soft Oriental silk was of deep rose-colour and it had a gold band inwoven in the material round the edges of the sari and the part which made up the long skirt. I wore the sari over my head and managed the clinging folds well enough.

But there was no doubt who was the belle of the ball. Cécile, a lovely and complacent Columbia, swam with swan-like grace, a queen among us all. She was draped in the star-spangled banner. An audacious *décolletage* showed her beautiful shoulders and the rise of her breast. Diamond stars crowned her and sparkled round her long slim throat. She was radiantly beautiful.

I was giving her her due of compliments, when Mlle Julie came up.

"*La belle Cécile!*" she cried. "You do us honour, *chère Amérique*—a beauty worthy of Lafayette's gallantry," she went on, laughing. "Turn round and let me look at you."

She put her hands on Cécile's bare arms and as she twisted her round, bent down and kissed her shoulder. A long deliberate kiss on the naked creamy shoulder. An unknown pang of astonishing violence stabbed me. I hated Cécile. I hated Mlle Julie. As she raised her eyes from the kiss, she saw me watching her. Had she noticed me before? I don't know. Now, I thought, she was mocking me.

"Is Olivia jealous of so much beauty?" she said. "No, Olivia, you'll never be beautiful, but you have your points," appraising me, I thought angrily, as if I had been an animal at a cattle show. "Pretty hands, pretty feet, a pretty figure, grace which is sometimes more than——" but then her voice trailed off into a murmur too low for me to hear. "But even if I wanted to kiss you, fair Indian, how could I, wrapped as you are in all those veils? Come though, I'll tell you a secret."

She drew me towards her, pulled back my sari, and whispered close, close in my ear, her lips almost touching me, her breath hot on my cheek:

"I'll come to-night and bring you a sweet."

She was gone.

I remember that I felt as if my whole frame had been turned to water. My knees were giving way. I had to cling to a table and support myself till I recovered strength enough to get to a chair—she was coming—to-night—in a few hours—— A paean sang in my heart. Had I been weak before? Now, exhilaration flowed through my veins. Why? Why? I didn't stop to think why. I only knew that there, in the immediate future, soon, soon, something was coming to me, some wild delight, some fierce anguish that my whole being called for. But I mustn't think of it. Now, I must dance. Just then Georgie passed me.

"Why are you so pale?" she asked and looked at me.

"Georgie," I said, "have you ever been in love?"

Georgie's dark eyes gloomed and glowed. I could see her breath quickening.

"Yes," she answered sombrely, "yes."

"And what's it like?"

"Too horrible to speak of." And then, as though some lovely memory were rising from the depths of her heart into the glowing eyes, they softened, melted, shone, behind a veil of tears—— "And too delicious—— Come, let's dance!"

She put her arm round me and pressed me to her. There was comfort in the contact. Comfort, I felt, and pleasure for us both. She was stronger, taller than I. My head could rest on her shoulder; I was conscious of hers bending over me.

Our steps, our limbs, harmonized, swayed, quickened, slackened to the music, as if one spirit informed them. I could trust myself to her guiding, I could abandon myself in a trance of ecstasy to the motion, to the rhythm, to the langours and the passions of the waltz.

That evening, we danced every waltz together (Georgie abandoned her grisette—"she can't dance for twopence"—), but we knew well enough that we were not dancing with each other, that one of us was clasping, the other being clasped by the phantom of her own dreams.

It was the fashion to end every ball with what was called a "galop". I don't think this dance exists nowadays. It was the tempestuous conclusion in those Victorian days to evenings that had been filled with sentimentalities and proprieties —waltzes and Lancers—and people would rush into the frenzy of rapid motion with a fury of excitement. When the waltzes were over that night, Nina and I, sped by some magnetic impulse, shot madly into each other's arms for the final galop. Excitement was in the air. Fräulein, at the piano, caught it too and added to it by the *brio* of her playing. But no couple could compete with Nina and me. We rushed and whirled, faster and faster, more and more furiously, our hair, our draperies, streaming like Maenads' behind us, till at last the others gave out exhausted and we were left whirling alone, the only couple on the floor. It was the music that surrendered first, and as, at last, we dropped to the ground, laughing and breathless, all the watching girls applauded.

The evening was over. It was time to go to bed. I should have been glad for it to last longer. There was something coming that I dreaded as much as I longed for it. I was approaching an abyss into which I was going to fall dizzy and shuddering. I averted my eyes, but I knew that it was there.

After all the noisy good-nights, I was at last alone in my room. I tore off my veils impatiently. I must make haste.

There was no time to be lost. I slipped into my schoolgirl's nightgown, high to the throat and buttoned to the wrists—and suddenly the vision of Cécile's creamy shoulder flashed upon me. I couldn't bear the hideous nightgown. I took out a clean day-chemise and put it on instead. That was better. My arms and neck at least were bare. I got into bed and blew out the candle.

What had she said? Pretty hands, pretty feet, a pretty figure. Yes, but in French, what strange expression does one use? "*Un joli corps.*" A pretty body. Mine, a pretty body. I had never thought of my body till that minute. A body! I had a body—and it was pretty. What was it like? I must look at it. There was still time. She wouldn't be coming yet. I lighted the candle, sprang out of bed and slipped off my chemise. The looking-glass—a small one—was over the wash-hand-stand. I could only see my face and shoulders in it. I climbed on to a chair. Then I could see more. I looked at the figure in the glass, queerly lighted, without head or legs, strangely attractive, strangely repulsive. And then I slowly passed my hands down this queer creature's body from neck to waist—Ah!—That was more than I could bear—that excruciating thrill I had never felt before. In a second my chemise was on again, I was back in bed.

And now, I listened, not thinking, not feeling any more, absorbed in listening. The noises gradually died away—slamming doors, footsteps, snatches of talk and laughter. The house was silent now. Not quite. I still heard from time to time a window or a shutter being closed or opened. Now. Yes, now it really was silent. Now was the time to hear a coming footstep, a creaking board. There! My heart beat, stood still, beat. No! A false alarm. How long she was! It must be getting late. How late! How late! And still she didn't come. She had never been as late as this before. I lighted my candle again and looked at my watch. One o'clock. And we had gone to bed at eleven. I crept to the door and opened it gently. I could see her room a little way off, on the opposite side of the passage. There was no light coming from the crack under the door. Nothing was stirring. Everything was wrapped in profound and deadly silence. I went heavily back to my bed. She had promised. She couldn't not come now. I must have faith in her. Or could anything have prevented her? Yet surely not for all this time. She knew I should wait for her. Ah! she was cruel. She had no right to promise and not to come. She had forgotten me. She didn't know whether I existed or not. She had other thoughts, other cares. Of course, of course. I was nothing to her. A silly schoolgirl. She liked Cécile better than she did me. Hark! A sound! Hope rose and died a dozen times that night. Even when I knew it was impossible—even when the late winter dawn was beginning to glimmer in the room, I still lay, tossing and listening. It must have been five o'clock before I fell asleep.

And yet I was to know other, bitterer vigils, during which I looked back on this one as happy—during which I realized she had never loved me, never would love me as well as on that night.

IX

I WAS awoken by Signorina standing by my bedside with a tray and breakfast on it.

"What time is it?" I asked.

"Ten o'clock. Orders were that you weren't to be called. You are to have breakfast in bed, but be ready at 10.45 to join the walk."

There was just time to breakfast and dress without thinking. I couldn't think during the walk either, and besides, I didn't want to. There was a visiting professor that day, so that I didn't sit beside her at lunch. I was glad of it. My morning's greeting was given with the others, as we all rose to our feet when the ladies entered the dining-room.

The day dragged on, but at about four o'clock someone came into the school-room and said:

"Olivia, you're wanted in the library. Mlle Julie's giving back the literature *devoirs*. Mine's not so bad this week. Hooray!"

I went with a sickened heart and faltering steps. A load of resentment, shame, humiliation, pressed me down.

She was sitting at the big writing-table in the middle of the room, a pile of copy-books before her.

"Sit down, *mon chéri*," she said. "Here's your *devoir*. There's no need to tell you, is there, that it's not at all good. You haven't been working well lately, Olivia." She sighed. How kind her voice was! How dreadfully sad! "Olivia," she went on, "you have many gifts and many graces. It would be a pity if you were to waste them all pursuing chimeras . . . *des chimères*!"

And then my swelling heart burst. I was tired; I was hopeless; I was resentful; I had been cheated; I had made a fool of myself; nothing was any good. *Chimères! Chimères!* I put my head down between my hands and sobbed.

She got up from her chair. Even through my fit of sobbing, I was intensely conscious of her movements. But she did not come near me. On the contrary, she walked away and stood by the fireplace.

"Olivia," she said gravely, "I'm sorry I disappointed you last night. If you don't understand why, I can't explain. But I would like you to understand this: I'm trying now to do the best for us." And then in a whisper, she added, so low that I could hardly hear it: *"Je t'aime bien, mon enfant."* Her voice broke and sank and then, lower still, she added, *"Plus que tu ne crois."* With that she was gone. The door shut and I was alone.

My sobs gradually died away in the stillness of the big room. The quiet, the deepening twilight, calmed me. The memory of her words, the tenderness of her voice, wrapped me round with a mantle of comfort. I dried my eyes. The great cast of the Victory of Samothrace glimmered white in a corner of the room; I could still see on one wall Michelangelo's prophets and sibyls, sitting robed in their majesty above me; on another, Piranesi's engraving of the Roman aqueduct led my eyes away into an infinity of grandeur; a bunch of Nice roses bloomed in a vase on the table; and all around me were books. Solemnity, nobility, beauty, love, were these then chimeras? No, no, a hundred times no! I believed in them. With my whole soul I believed in them. It was no waste of gifts and graces to pursue them. But I must pursue them in a purer spirit, with more faith, with less selfishness. It would be easier now. I was no longer alone. She was with me— beside me. She had said "us". She had lifted me to her star. She loved me too, better than—ah! infinitely better than I deserved. She, with her own greater sorrows, had spared time to be sorry for me. Pity and gratitude flooded me, overpowered me. I drooped beneath them. How tired I was! I took a cushion from the armchair on which she usually sat, put it on the floor, sank my head down on it and fell asleep.

I don't know how long it was before I woke to find the light turned on and Mlle Cara standing over me.

"You!" she said, "and what are you doing here?"

Half dazed, I sat up, blinked my eyes and answered, "Nothing. I was asleep."

"Asleep!" she said angrily. "And how do you come to be asleep here of all the places in the world?"

I rose to my feet, muttered vaguely, "I'm sorry," and tried to make for the door.

But she caught hold of me and began to pour forth a torrent of agitated, incoherent words:

"You! You, whom I had hoped for, whom I had looked forward to—you too betray me, abandon me. What would your mother say if she knew? If she knew how you were being led astray, demoralized, depraved? How idle you have become, and for all I know, vicious! Fallen into the hands of a low-born Italian Jewess—and into others, worse, worse! Look at you now, your hair down, your dress so untidy and rumpled, your eyes wild! Shame on you, Olivia! Shame! Shame!"

Her voice rose to a shriek. I thought she was demented. I had never seen a person in hysterics before. I was terrified by that shrill choking, sobbing laughter, by those insane words. And suddenly she turned. Mlle Julie had come into the room behind me; I was standing now between the two.

"What is it, Cara?" she said.

The raving flood changed its direction and went on. She was shaking now from head to foot.

"One of your favourites, one of your darlings, one of your *victims*!" she shrieked.

"Go, Olivia," said Mlle Julie.

She managed to extricate me and I ran to the door, but before I reached it, I heard the fury cry:

"Oh yes, you go to their rooms at night—Cécile's, Baietto's and now hers! You do, you *do*."

My brain was whirling. I too was trembling from head to foot. What did it all mean? Why did I suddenly feel as if I were surrounded by horrors, as if the landscape, which a moment before had shone with an almost celestial radiance, were clouded now with darkness, full of abominable pitfalls and lurking hideous monsters? Mystery was about me, murky suspicions, and, at the bottom of my heart lay jealousy such as I had never known before, and a dreadful curiosity and a dreadful longing for wickedness. In so short a time to be cast from the glories of Paradise into this direful region! It was the first time I learnt how near, how contiguous, are the gates of Heaven and Hell.

That night too I slept very little. I lay for hours, it seemed to me, tossing in an aimless conflict, everything at war within me, every issue confused and shadowy. What was this vice of which I was accused? Was I really capable of vice? Yes, I felt it within me, in this hatred, in this horror, in this confusion itself. But love was no vice. When best I loved, then I was best. But lately, had not love too been clouded with exhalations from some obscure depths, at which I shuddered? Why were good and evil so inextricably mixed? Evil? Was there any evil in my love's pure face, in the sweetness of her sensitive lips, in the delicate, pale curve of her cheek, in the deep thoughtful eyes, in the grave brow? And I thought of the other face, distorted with anger, swollen, inflamed, with

ugly hatreds, ugly vanities, ugly weaknesses. Was there any
doubt where virtue lay between those two? And then my
thoughts were punctuated again by the sudden, flashing vision
of Cécile's creamy shoulder, and I writhed in my bed—I too
in the clutches of ugly hatreds, ugly vanities, ugly weaknesses.
I should like to pray, thought I, if only I knew to what deity.
Ah! It is Reason I must implore—some calm Minerva, who
shall look down from her god-like abode, and still my passions, and dispel these sulphurous fumes, and restore to my
soul clarity and discernment. And with the thought and with
the prayer, peace fell on me and I slept.

X

I SPRANG out of bed next morning, full of good resolutions, determined to work better, to love better, to *be* better. I would attend to the history professor, though he *was* dull. I would check my thoughts the moment they began to wander down the familiar alluring paths. I would concentrate my mind on what I had to do. I would do it as well as I could. Alas! I had not yet learnt that concentration of mind comes from long discipline and sternly acquired habit. On the very first morning of what was to be my new life, how could I expect to banish entirely those haunting visions—of a shoulder —of a profile? Was I responsible when, in the middle of the professor's lecture, his voice, his words, his person, were suddenly obliterated and I was conscious of nothing but an almost inaudible murmur, "*Je t'aime bien mon enfant . . . plus que tu ne crois.*"? Could I help it, if, with a sudden wild leap of my heart, I felt my lips pressing against warm hands, the hardness of a ring, the roughness of a woollen dress? Or again, if I heard a frantic voice cry, "You go to Cécile's room at night!" I would try to suppress these feelings, these suspicions, by forcing an interest in Richelieu's government—was it my fault if I failed?

These anxieties and suspicions broke their way to the surface during my Italian lesson.

"Signorina," I asked (but I despised myself as I asked it), "Is it true she goes to Cécile's room at night?"

"To Cécile's room!" laughed Signorina, "Why on earth should she go there? She doesn't care two straws for Cécile. And as for Cécile, if her beauty-sleep were disturbed, she'ld certainly leave the very next morning. Mlle Cara's been at you, I see."

There was a pause. Then she went on: "Olivia," she said, "she comes to me as well as to you, because we love her. And I think I have more reason to be jealous of you than you of me. But I'm not. She talks to me. She tells me about this dreadful situation. She told me last night about the scene Mlle Cara had with you. She said she was like a madwoman. . . . It can't go on. It's bad for everyone, bad for the school, for the girls. It's eating the heart out of her. And all she does to pacify Mlle Cara only makes her worse. She has finally made up her mind. She has decided to leave."

"To leave!" I cried aghast. "How? When? What will she do?"

"Nothing is settled," answered Signorina, but she thinks she'll let Frau Riesener and Mlle Cara carry on here and that she'll go to Canada and start a fresh school there. I shall go with her, of course."

It seems hard to believe, but this was the very first time I had ever thought of the future. I had been so utterly absorbed by the newness and violence of all my emotions, that it had never occurred to me the present could be anything but eternal. It was of myself I thought first. She was going—to Canada—to another world—— She was going, perhaps for ever—— Immeasurable oceans would separate me from her —immeasurable ages——

I grew dizzy with the shock. The world swam. A cloud of darkness came over my eyes. I think I was on the point of fainting.

There was a sofa in the little study where we had our Italian lessons. Signorina made me lie down on it. I was thankful for this bodily weakness, which, like an anaesthetic, dulled an intolerable pain. Vaguely, I felt that I had heard something cruel, something frightful, but when, what, I didn't know. Signorina took up *I Promessi Sposi* and began reading aloud in a monotonous voice. I let the melodious Italian sounds flow over me, lap me round, as I lay there on the sofa, not listening, not thinking. Then, suddenly I became conscious again.

"Oh, Signorina," I cried, sitting up and stretching out my hands to her, "What shall I do? How shall I bear it?"

"Try to be calmer, Olivia." (Oh, these grown-ups! Calmer!) "There's no need to be agitated just yet. Everything will go on just the same to the end of the term. And in any case, you would be going home for the holidays. I don't suppose you need come back next term, when she's not here."

(Come back next term, when she's not here!)

"And then, Olivia, I've planned it all out. We shall have a school in Canada and in two or three years' time, you'll be old enough, you'll have passed your examinations, and you'll come out and be a teacher in the new school."

(In two or three years! ! !)

Vain, idle consolations! I knew it.

So now, if the beak and talons of the vulture jealousy had eased their grip on my heart, another worse torment was mine. I became conscious of the flight of time. Five weeks! And soon there would be four, and soon three, and soon two, and soon only one, and then . . .

I was the prisoner condemned to execution. There was no escape. I turned and turned in my cage. No thought of submission, no thought of acceptance touched me, very little thought of anyone else's sufferings but my own. Yes, I was the prisoner of my own selfishness. And the more I longed to stay the inexorable passage of the days, the faster, the more terrifyingly they fled. I had scarcely left my bedroom in the morning than I was back again in it at night. One more of the precious days had gone by beyond recall and left nothing behind it, not one grain of gold to add to my tiny heap of treasure. During all those days, Mlle Julie was kind to me, but distant. I no longer dared to go unbidden to the library.

She no longer dropped her hand into mine, if we chanced to be alone; and if I listened to her footsteps down the passage on the nights she came in late, it was no longer with the beating heart of hope.

During all those days too, the signs of approaching change, of approaching catastrophe even, were becoming more and more visible. I had been told by Signorina to say nothing of the coming break, and I did not, but there was uneasiness in the air. Girls whispered in corners; mistresses looked anxious. There were unusual comings and goings. Gentlemen with black *serviettes* full of papers were closeted upstairs with the ladies in the *cabinet de travail*. Mlle Julie went oftener to Paris, and one day, even Mlle Cara herself, wrapped up in shawls and mufflers and accompanied by Frau Riesener, drove out (to the town, it was said), in a closed carriage.

"They are making legal arrangements," said Signorina. "A deed of separation has to be drawn up. She is being far too generous to Mlle Cara. Frau Riesener sees to it that her dear friend gets every ounce she can extract. And Mlle Julie doesn't care. It was she who put every penny of capital into the school, but she's getting very little back. And, what do you think, when she stipulated she should have her father's books, they said they must be valued and half the value put to Mlle Cara's credit. She just shrugged her shoulders and consented."

And so these odious questions of material interest had to be debated when hearts were breaking.

When hearts were breaking . . .

One evening was generally set apart during the week for Mlle Julie to read to the elder girls in the library. Those evenings have coloured for me all French literature. How many masterpieces she read us! How many she clothed in the beauty of her voice! How many she passed on to us, infused and vivified by the zest of her wit, by the spirit of her genius.

Ah, Bérénice! Can I ever think of your heart-rending majesty without hearing her intonation, without seeing her grey eyes and the quiver of her lips as she spoke the simple, immortal words of farewell?

> ——*Et pour jamais adieu!*
> *Pour jamais! Ah! Seigneur, songez-vous en vous-même*
> *Combien ce mot cruel est affreux quand on aime?*
> *Dans un mois, dans un an, comment souffrirons-nous,*
> *Seigneur, que tant de mers me séparent de vous,*
> *Que le jour recommence et que le jour finisse*
> *Sans que jamais Titus puisse voir Bérénice,*
> *Sans que de tout le jour je puisse voir Titus?*

Alceste and Célimène! it is thanks to her that you live in my life, and you too, dear, worthy Monsieur Jourdain, and you, Don Rodrigue! Often as I say to myself the opening stanza of *Le Lac*, it is never without remembering the lilt, the rapid horror and rush of her utterance in the first three lines, the slow knell-like toll of the last four monosyllables:

> *Ainsi, toujours poussés vers de nouveaux rivages,*
> *Dans la nuit éternelle emportés sans retour,*
> *Ne pourrons-nous jamais sur l'océan des âges*
> > *Jeter l'ancre un seul jour?*

I remember the last time I heard her read aloud. It was our evening. She had missed several of late, but this time she did not miss it. There were six or seven of us. I did not take a seat near her but where I could see her face, and this time, as on that first evening so long ago, she was holding her ivory paper-cutter, and as on that first evening, she called me up to sit beside her:

"Come, Olivia, sit here."

But of all that she read that evening, I remember only one poem: *Paroles sur la Dune.*

Oh, if in my egoism, I have drawn a picture of myself rather than of her, let those who read me remember how distant she was from me, what a different world of experience and emotion she inhabited, how difficult, how almost impossible it was for me to imagine what she was suffering! Let them listen again to those tragic, heavy words, so weighted with memory, regret, remorse, and realize that I came near to understanding them!

> *Maintenant que mon temps décroît comme un flambeau,*
>   *Que mes tâches sont terminées;*
> *Maintenant que voici que je touche au tombeau*
>   *Par les deuils et par les années*
>
> * * *
>
> *Où donc s'en sont allés mes jours évanouis?*
>   *Est-il quelqu'un qui me connaisse?*
> *Ai-je encor quelque chose en mes yeux éblouis,*
>   *De la clarté de ma jeunesse?*
>
> * * *
>
> *Ne verrai-je plus rien de tout ce que j'aimais?*
>   *Au dedans de moi le soir tombe.*
> *O terre, dont la brume efface les sommets,*
>   *Suis-je le spectre, et toi la tombe?*
>
> *Ai-je donc vidé tout, vie, amour, joie, espoir?*
>   *J'attends, je demande, j'implore;*
> *Je penche tour à tour mes urnes pour avoir*
>   *De chacune une goutte encore!*
>
> *Comme le souvenir est voisin du remord!*
>   *Comme à pleurer tout nous ramène!*
> *Et que je te sens froide en te touchant, ô mort,*
>   *Noir verrou de la porte humaine!*

It was to me she was reading. I knew it. Yes, I understood, but no one else did. Once more that sense of profound intimacy, that communion beyond the power of words or caresses to bestow, gathered me to her heart. I was with her, beside her, for ever close to her, in that infinitely lovely, infinitely distant star, which shed its mingled rays of sorrow, affection and renouncement on the dark cold world below.

XI

THE next day, Mlle Julie went to Paris; she hoped to be back for dinner; she wasn't sure.

We gathered that Mlle Cara had one of her bad migraines. Frau Riesener was in and out of her room all day, looking after her. She was to have a sleeping-draught at night—the usual thing in those days, before tabloids or cachets were invented. We were told to creep to bed as quietly as possible so as not to disturb her.

"Frau Riesener's tired," Signorina said to me after dinner. "She has gone to bed too and she wants me to prepare the draught and give it to Mlle Cara. But I'm not going to. I've told her she'd better give Miss Smith instructions. She's quite trustworthy."

Early in bed, I dozed off and slept restlessly for two or three hours. Once I thought I heard footsteps in the passage and listened eagerly. But no; it was some one else, and I didn't hear Mlle Julie's carriage drive up till much later. I looked at my watch; it was nearly twelve. Then my listening began. I must hear her walk past my door before I should be able to sleep again. She delayed a shorter time than usual that night, and sooner than I expected I heard her step at the end of the long corridor. Rapid at first, it became slower and slower as it drew near, seemed to be faltering, came to a stop. She was outside my door. The handle turned and she came in. I could hardly see her in the dark. She came up to my bed and sat down on it. My arms were round her neck, my head on her shoulder. She pressed me to her.

"I'm tired; I'm weak," she murmured. Then almost passionately, but below her breath, she cried:

"My purest joys have been spoilt. Even my thoughts have

been spoilt. Even my inmost self. But I have no joys now. I must say goodbye now to everything I have loved. To you too, Olivia, Olivia."

She bent her head to kiss me and I felt her tears on my cheek.

And so I lay a moment longer in her arms, my head upon her shoulder, weeping too.

Only a moment. She disengaged herself gently, and as I still clung desperately to her hands, holding them to my heart, she said, almost sternly, "Let me go, Olivia."

I obeyed.

As the door closed behind her, I lay down in my bed and buried my face in my pillow.

*   *   *   *   *

But what was this that suddenly disturbed me? What frightful clamour? My door was flung violently open. Mlle Julie was standing there, a candle in her hand, terror on her face.

"Quick! Quick!" she cried in a hoarse, unrecognizable voice, "Go and fetch Signorina and Frau Riesener. Something's the matter with Mlle Cara. Run! Run!"

I dashed out of bed and without stopping to put on dressing-gown or slippers sped down the dark passage, up the stairs, which were dimly lighted by nightlights top and bottom, and flung open Signorina's door. I knew she would be awake.

"Quick! Quick!" I cried breathlessly, "There's something the matter—— Mlle Julie—— Mlle Cara—— She wants you."

Signorina was out of bed, clutching me.

"The matter with whom?" she cried.

"Mlle Cara. Mlle Cara. I must go now and call Frau Riesener."

She held me back. "What is it? What is it?"

"I don't know. Go to her quick."

Again I tore along the passage to Frau Riesener's room at the other end. I had a harder task there. I knocked at the door; I almost battered on it. Then I opened it and called:

"Frau Riesener! Frau Riesener! Wake up! Wake up! Wake up!"

"What is it?" she said at last.

"You're wanted downstairs. Quick!—— Mlle Cara—— There's something the matter."

I saw her light the candle deliberately.

"What is it?" she said again.

"I don't know—I don't know, I tell you. But you're wanted—quick—quick!"

When I got downstairs again, Signorina was there in her neat little dressing-gown and slippers, bustling about with hot-water bottles, hot cloths and so on, and she was soon joined by Frau Riesener. I was despatched to wake the house-keeper and tell her to send for the doctor, but first Signorina made me put on a skirt, a woollen coat and shoes.

"What has happened?" I asked.

"An overdose of chloral," was the answer, as I knew it would be.

"And how is she?"

"Unconscious. That's all I can say. We can't do anything more till the doctor comes."

But in those days, there were no telephones, no motor-cars. The gardener's boy would go to the town on his bicycle; the doctor would drive out in his carriage. An hour must elapse at the very least before he could possibly arrive. I stayed in my room, waiting, not daring to enquire, sometimes standing at my door listening, sometimes restlessly walking up and down my little bedroom, or lying face downwards on my bed. After the first confusion and agitation, the bustle died away and was succeeded by a deathly silence.

Once, kind little Signorina put her head into my room for a second, but all she said was, "No change." I saw no more of Mlle Julie.

At last I heard the doctor's step, a brief, whispered colloquy in the passage between him and Frau Riesener, the sound of a gently shutting door. I nerved myself for another long wait. There would certainly be all kinds of things to do—emetics, stomach-pumps, artificial breathing. I imagined all this, but no. Dreadful as the delay of his coming had been, the shortness of his stay was more dreadful still. I heard him and Frau Riesener walking down the passage together. It was he who was talking this time.

Signorina came to my room then.

"I can only stay a second, Olivia. It's all over. She's dead. She's been dead for hours."

I don't know how I got through the night. This was no personal grief, but I was hardly aware of that. It was my first contact with death and death with some of its worst terrors, unexpected, unapprehended—the brutal stroke of some awful, malignant power lying in wait for us, ready to pounce when we were least prepared. Not the slow natural death of elders, not the anticipated, inevitable result of disease, but an accident. An avoidable, unnecessary accident. An accident! But was it an accident? A fresh horror chilled me. Supposing it were *not* an accident. Supposing she had taken the overdose on purpose? Could she have? No, it was impossible. Why should she do such a thing? And yet I knew she had often threatened to. But then I had heard that people who threatened never did it—it was a common saying. And nobody had ever seemed to take her threats seriously. It must be an accident. Miss Smith was to pour out the dose for her. She had made a mistake. Professor Tyndall, I remembered, had died in that very way from an overdose of chloral given him by his wife, who had nearly gone mad with grief afterwards. What were the others thinking? Mlle Julie? Oh! let me turn away my thoughts from her? Signorina? Frau Riesener? And the doctor? Should I ever know what had happened? Would they tell me? Would they know themsleves?

*　　*　　*　　*　　*

Though I think that, thanks to Signorina, I was told in the course of the next few days all the conclusions that were come to, I still imagine that I was never told their real suspicions. At any rate, I never told mine. There was, of course, an enquiry the next day. The doctor, the *commissaire de police*, some odd gentlemen called "the *parquet*" were constantly in the house. Everybody remotely connected with the affair was questioned. I myself was summoned to give an account of what I knew. I was particularly questioned as to the hour of Mlle Julie's return and how I knew it was at twelve o'clock midnight, as I stated.

"Because I heard her carriage drive up and looked at my watch."

"How do you know it was her carriage?"

"Because she came to my room."

"Ah? And why was that?" They raised their brows and I hated them.

I cast about for some lie. How could one desecrate the truth by telling it to people like them?

"I'd not been very well that morning and she came to ask how I was and whether I wanted anything."

"And did she say anything particular?"

(Anything particular!)

"No. She just said 'How are you?' and 'Good-night!'"

(Fortunately Mlle Julie must have said much the same, for they made no comment.)

"And how long after that was it that she called you?"

"About two minutes, I should think."

"Thank you, Mademoiselle. That will do."

Frau Riesener was questioned as to Mlle Cara's mental condition.

"Perfectly calm and cheerful," was the answer. Though she had had a headache in the morning, and had not slept well the night before, she seemed better in the evening, and when Frau Riesener had said good-night to her at about eight o'clock, she had advised her not to take the sleeping-draught. 'Oh!' she had said, 'I'll just have it put beside me and not take it unless I feel I'm not going to sleep.' Frau Riesener had had a bad headache herself, had given her instructions to Miss Smith, and then gone to bed.

Miss Smith was then asked whether she agreed that Mlle Cara was in a calm, cheerful state of mind?

"No, anything but," was her answer.

"Did she say anything in particular?"

"She moaned a good deal about her headache."

"Is that all?"

"Once she said——"

"Yes? What?"

" 'I wish I hadn't done it.' "

"Done what?"

"I don't know. I've no idea."

When asked about the dose, Miss Smith swore with tears that she had poured out the exact dose, as instructed by Frau Riesener, and put it on Mlle Cara's bedside table.

Frau Riesener swore (without tears) that she had instructed her to give the exact dose prescribed by the doctor.

The doctor swore that if that were so, no fatal result could possibly have ensued.

The bottle was produced. Miss Smith had put it back in the medicine chest that same evening. Was the medicine chest kept locked? Yes, generally. But that evening Frau Riesener, who kept the key as a rule, had given it to Miss

Smith who, not thinking it necessary to disturb Frau Riesener by returning it the same night, had left it in the lock.

There was conflicting evidence over the bottle. When full, it contained six doses. Two *might* be fatal to a person of Mlle Cara's constitution. It was a bottle on which the doses were divided off by lines. When produced, it was shown that there were three doses left. Frau Riesener swore that when she gave it to Miss Smith, it contained five doses. Miss Smith swore, with tears, that it had contained only four—and then she grew flustered and confused, and said that perhaps, after all, there had been five doses, but she was positively sure she had poured the medicine out to the exact line shown her by Frau Riesener.

Frau Riesener was ready to prove that there were five doses in the bottle when she gave it to Miss Smith. She had only given Mlle Cara one dose out of that bottle. She always noted these things in her diary. There it was! A fortnight before, Mlle Cara had had a dose and none in the interval. Therefore five doses had been in the bottle when she had given it to Miss Smith.

At the end of this agitated day, the doctor signed a certificate to say *Death by misadventure, caused by accidentally taking an overdose of chloral,* and the *commissaire* and the *parquet* accepted his finding without demur. The ladies were highly esteemed in the town; Frau Riesener and the doctor were on the best of terms and very willing to exonerate each other. Nobody wanted to make the business more disagreeable than was necessary for anyone—except for the unfortunate Miss Smith. Nothing, however, could be clearer. It was a deplorable mistake, but there it was. There was no further enquiry —no post-mortem. Only the slightest allusion was made to the coming separation between the friends. Mlle Julie, as Signorina admitted, had been treated with the utmost consideration and sympathy by everyone.

But as I myself pondered over the affair, I came to the conclusion that *ces Messieurs de la police et du parquet* had done their work very inefficiently, and very unfairly for poor little Miss Smith. Even the doctor, I thought, was to blame. Several possibilities occurred to me which had not been gone into: perhaps her heart was weak and one dose had sufficed to kill her. The doctor had refused to consider the possibility of this—it would have been a proof of his negligence had it been the case.

The medicine chest had been admittedly left open that night; it stood in the *lingerie* at the end of the passage, a door or two from Mlle Cara's room. What was there to prevent her from going to it and taking the extra dose herself?

For that matter, *anyone* might have gone to the cupboard and taken the bottle and poured the extra dose into the glass —anyone who had access to Mlle Cara's room. But this was a fantastic idea!

"Mlle Julie is afraid, I can see, that she did it herself. But I'm absolutely certain," said Signorina stoutly, "that she didn't. She was incapable of such a thing. And at any rate she wouldn't have done it like that. She'ld have made the most of it—left a farewell note—done it theatrically—and probably managed after all to be brought round before it was too late."

"What did she mean by saying, 'I wish I hadn't done it'?"

"I've thought and thought and I can't imagine. At any rate," she went on, "I thank my stars that I refused to pour out the dose myself, as Frau Riesener wanted me to. I should have been landed perhaps, in poor Miss Smith's shoes."

"Oh no, Signorina, you wouldn't. You'ld never have made the mistake."

She smiled grimly: "Perhaps not."

None of my doubts were ever solved with any certainty.

I still sometimes puzzle over them. I am still constantly baffled. Psychological or material objections seem to block the way to every solution, and yet the solution, we know, exists; it is there, like a lost jewel, close at hand perhaps, if only some power would give us eyes to see it.

XII

WHAT with the enquiry and the last offices that had to be rendered to the poor dead body, the day passed busily enough, I suppose, for everybody. Signorina did her best to occupy me too. The school, as may be imagined, had been thrown into a state of consternation and disorganization. There were no classes, no walks; huddled groups collected in corners; nothing was heard but hushed whispers; no girl dared look at another as they passed tip-toeing along the passages. The shadow of death was on us all.

"You must occupy the little ones, Olivia," said Signorina. "Take them into the study and read to them after tea."

It was the kindest thing she could have done for me. I often read to the little ones; they enjoyed it and so did I. We had a book in hand—*Ivanhoe*, I think. Reading aloud forced me to a certain surface attention, without putting too great a strain on my mind. The back of my mind was still busy with the tragedy upstairs, but I could not let it absorb me. And the little ones that evening were very charming, I thought.

"A cushion for Olivia."

"A stool for Olivia."

"I'm going to sit next her."

"So am I."

"Isn't it wrong to listen to a story?" asked one.

"No, it's quite right. It's the best thing you can do to help every one."

"Does it help you?"

"Oh yes. Me most of all."

"Then we'll listen. Go on. Go on."

And at the end they clustered round me to thank me, to kiss me. They flung their arms round my neck; they stroked my cheek. One of them said, I remember, "Poor pretty.

Olivia," and it was all I could do to keep from crying. And so the evening went by. But the night was to follow—the first night of vigil.

Signorina came to my room at about ten o'clock, looking, I thought, wild-eyed.

"She won't let me stay with her," she said. "She won't have anyone with her. She got angry with me when I implored her to let me stay, if only in the next room. 'She was *my* friend,' she said. She said it almost fiercely, Olivia. 'She was the only person I ever loved, and am I not to spend the first night alone with her? To-morrow, you and Frau Riesener can do as you please, but to-night I'm going to be alone.' When she talks in that voice, I daren't disobey. But oh, her face is terrible."

We clung to each other for a moment or two and then she went slowly and heavily away.

At eleven o'clock, I could bear it no longer. I put on my dressing-gown and slippers and crept out of my room. Everything was silent, everything dark, except for a ray of light that came from underneath the door of Mlle Cara's room. A dressing-room separated it from Mlle Julie's. Oh, I had no thought of intruding on that vigil, but I must spend it near her. I sat down on the floor outside the door, as I had seen Indian servants sit and sleep outside their masters' rooms, my knees drawn up, my arms clasped round them, my head resting on them. I could sit so for a long time. Sometimes I dozed, sometimes I thought of her. What was she suffering? What were her regrets, her memories—remorse too, perhaps. I remembered that verse she had read:

Comme le souvenir est voisin du remord!

What could I do for her? How could I help her, how serve her? There was nothing I could do. Each of us must suffer alone. Alone! How alone she was in there! Alone with a dead body—with the only person she had ever loved. A dead past behind her. A dreary future of exile before her. . . . But perhaps now that exile would not be necessary. Perhaps she would be able to stay on here, recover, be happy again. I should be with her; Signorina too; life would smile once more. And so my thoughts wandered and I built a shining, flimsy fabric and then came to myself with a shudder of horror. There was a dead body behind that door, and I was thinking already of happiness.

Mlle Cara—I must turn my thoughts to her. What had her life been? Unhappiness had come to her too. She too had been wounded perhaps in her deepest soul. She too had been wounded perhaps by the person she loved best. And so that was what love led to. To wound and be wounded. I myself was on the same bitter road. No. I would not believe it. Out of such suffering, if only we could have strength to use it rightly, virtue might be fashioned. Poor Mlle Cara had been weak, vain, selfish—so I judged—she had been deteriorated by suffering, she had given way, she had let herself be devoured by jealousy and vanity. Could she have helped it? I didn't know; but Mlle Julie had helped it and so would I. I would be better for my love, for my pain. Even the pain of absence—so I vowed with clenched teeth—should make me better not worse. What did *better* and *worse* mean? Oh, that was too difficult a question for just now. It was enough to say that I felt what they meant—and that I chose with all my heart to be on the side of good.

I had clenched my teeth and now I felt that they were chattering. I was cold.

I tried to remember the end of the verse that had been ringing in my head:

> *Comme le souvenir est voisin du remord !*
> *Comme à pleurer tout nous ramène !*

What came after that?

Et que je te sens froide en te touchant, ô mort,
Noir verrou de la porte humaine!

Cold! Cold! I was dreadfully cold. I was shivering. I thought of my bed and blankets. What was I doing here? Why didn't I go back to them? What use was I here? None. None whatever, But no; some violent compulsion forbade me to go. I must watch out the night with her. I would stay here till dawn broke, however cold, however perishing I felt. I must not abandon her. A strange feeling that my staying was of vital importance had taken hold of me. I must stay. I must stay. The cold crept up me, from feet to legs; arms, shoulders, were cold, icy. I rubbed myself, but it was no good. I couldn't think any more. I was possessed of only two sensations—this cold and the desperate, blind determination to stay. I wouldn't even get up. No, though I was numb and stiff, if I got up, if I moved, I should be tempted; I should desert my post; I should fail. I would not fail. The time went by slowly, very slowly. But I could not see my watch. There was no light.

Suddenly I heard a sound. It was quite close to me. It was at my ear. It was the rattle of the door-handle, and before I had time to realize what was happening, the door opened and Mlle Julie stood there, a candle in her hand. She almost stumbled over me.

"What is that?" she cried. "Who is it?"

She stooped her face to look at me. It was strangely lighted by the candle.

"Olivia!" she said. "What are you doing there? Get up! Speak!"

I tried to, but I couldn't. I was too numb to move. My teeth were chattering so that I couldn't speak.

She helped me up, put her arm round me—for I needed her support, and cried, "Heavens! How cold you are! You must come and get warmed. Come."

She drew me into the room. There, on the bed, was the figure. I shivered still more when I saw it.

"Don't be afraid, my dear. Look! There's nothing terrible in the sight." And now she led me to the bed and held my hand as I looked. No, it was not terrible—a sweet face, calm and gentle. But the colour! I had always heard them speak of the waxen, the ivory pallor of death. But this face, I thought, was yellow. A horrible nausea seized me and, "I'm going to be sick," I cried desperately.

In an instant, Mlle Julie's arm was round me again. She supported me, dragged me through the dressing-room into the next room and put me in an armchair beside a fire. As quick as lightning, there was a basin in front of me and I was indeed being violently sick. She was very swift and sure in her movements. An eiderdown quilt was tucked round my knees, shawls wrapped round my shoulders in a moment; the basin was removed as soon as possible; eau-de-Cologne dabbed on my dank, cold forehead; there was a kettle of boiling water on the hearth and a hot-water bottle put to my feet, and a hot grog with a stiff spoonful of brandy in it to my lips; then she knelt down beside me, chafed my frozen hands, chafed even my feet, murmuring to herself as she did so, "Poor child! Poor child!" This went on as it seemed to me for a long time, and for a long time my teeth continued to chatter, but at last a delicious warmth crept over me, drowsiness weighted my eyelids, and, hardly knowing where I was, except that I was in comfort, my head sank on to her shoulder and I slept.

*   *   *   *   *

When I woke up it was dawn. I raised my head from the

pillow on which it was resting and looked about me. I was in her room. I had never been in it before. This was where she slept. There was her bed. It had not been slept in, and if it was disordered, it was because the blankets and eiderdown had been taken from it to wrap round me, and the pillow to put under my head. She herself, dressed in a long woollen wrapper, was standing at the window, her back towards me. Slowly the memory of the night before came back to me and the memory of Mlle Cara's figure lying next door. Mlle Julie heard me stirring and turned round. She smiled.

"Better, Olivia? Yes, you're quite rosy this morning. You must go back to your room now."

I was beginning to collect myself, when I saw there was something she wanted to say to me. She seemed to be making a great effort. I saw her wet her lips once or twice as if they were too dry for her to be able to speak. Then, in a curious, colourless voice, she said:

"Perhaps you'll like to hear that I think you saved my life last night. When I stumbled over you in the passage, I was going to the medicine chest. There are three doses left in the bottle. Mlle Baietto was careful to see that the cupboard was locked and to take away the key herself. I expect she's sleeping with it under her pillow. She didn't know I had a duplicate."

I had thrown aside my blankets and ran to kneel before her.

"And now?" I asked.

"Now?" she answered. "No, you needn't be afraid now. I saw last night that one can't kill oneself without killing too many other things beside. I've done enough harm in my life already."

She bent her head near to mine, but she did not touch me.

"Believe, Olivia, believe," she said earnestly, solemnly, "I don't want to harm you."

Kneeling before her, I took her hand religiously in mine and kissed it, with nothing now in my heart but the very purity of pity.

As I was leaving the room, she called after me:

"You're to stay in bed all day to-day. We must make sure you haven't caught bronchitis. Take my shawl with you."

I did as she told me, went to my room and to my bed, stiff, aching in every limb, but scandalously, intolerably happy.

XIII

I STAYED in bed all that day and did not catch pneumonia, bronchitis, or even a cold in my head. I think it was because I was too happy. Signorina, busy as she was, visited me often, looking at me, I thought, curiously, and perhaps enviously.

It was settled, she told me, that the school should break up for the holidays at once (only a fortnight was wanting to the end of the term). With girls who came from so many different countries, and often had long journeys to make, difficult and complicated arrangements had to be made for accompanying them and insuring they should be met, so that it was impossible to get rid of them before the funeral. That was to be on the next day—Thursday. Frau Riesener was seeing to it and helping with the *lettres de faire part*, of which there were hundreds to be sent, without counting the more intimate letters to friends. Mlle Julie herself wrote only three or four.

"And is the day on which the English girls are to go home settled?"

"Yes," she answered gently. "Saturday. Saturday morning. Miss Smith is to take you."

"Oh, Signorina," I said, "need she still go to Canada? What is she meaning to do? Can't she stop on here now?"

"I don't know. She has said nothing about it so far. We must wait for the will."

"The will?" I gasped.

"Yes," said Signorina. "All the deeds of separation had been signed some days ago. The house and contents were made absolutely over to Mlle Cara, in consideration of an annuity to be paid to Mlle Julie—far too low a one, but there it is. So now it remains to be seen whether Mlle Cara had made a will and in that case to whom she has left her property. I expect Frau Riesener has taken pretty good care of that."

My flimsy, shining fabric fell shattered to the ground. I knew now what was coming. It was not a foreboding, but a certainty.

On Thursday, the day of the funeral, the girls and governesses were sent out for a long walk and picnic. They had to be got out of the way. A dismal picnic it was, but a lull, a parenthesis, between past and future anguish. The sun was shining; the air was mild; the forest was beginning to put on its mist of green, and the earliest flowers were pushing up their heads through last year's decayed leaves as on the day of my first walk in it so many ages ago. Edith, Gertrude and I walked and talked together in low subdued voices; I was half-absent from the conversation, but yet I was glad to be with my friends.

I knew what was awaiting me when I got in, and yet when the blow fell, it was as though I had been unprepared for it. As soon as Signorina was able to speak to me alone, she told me that the will had been found and read, and that Mlle Cara had left all her property absolutely to Frau Riesener, who was only subjected to the condition of the annuity.

"That day they went out in the carriage, it was to go to the *notaire's* and sign the will—just two days before the accident. So now," she added, "that woman has got what she wanted. She is triumphant, sole mistress of the school, freed from the persons she detested—and even," she added sardonically, "from the one she loved."

Queer fragments of thought came into my mind, like bits of a jig-saw puzzle, which, when I had time, I might perhaps piece together, but now I brushed them away:

"And the Canada plan, does it still hold good?"

"I think so," she said. "But Mlle Julie seems to be in a kind of torpor still. She won't talk to me about anything."

And yet I felt that Signorina was triumphant too. She too was left in sole possession of the field. "In Canada," she was singing to herself, or so I guessed, "in Canada, I shall be alone with her, her only friend, her only help, her only servant."

The next day was Friday, and we English girls were told to pack. We were to leave by an early train the following morning. In the afternoon, Mlle Julie would say good-bye to us. We, of her class, were assembled in the little study and were summoned one by one to the library, where she was waiting for us. Two or three of the girls came back weeping. Each was holding a book—her parting present. "She was so kind," they sobbed. "She looked so sad, so desolate, in her big armchair."

I had made up my mind that I should be called last. I dreamt that in any case it wouldn't be the final farewell. She would come once more to my room to-night, to-night.

Four of the girls had gone to their interview. There were two more to go and then it would be my turn. I counted them. I calculated the minutes. I looked at the clock. I listened to its ticking—the slow unrelenting footfall of time.

But when the fourth girl came back, she said, "Olivia, you're to go next."

I have known what it is to wait in a surgeon's waiting-room. I have imagined what it is to enter his consulting-room in expectation of a sentence of death. Some of those feelings, I think, were mine—that swimming giddiness of body and soul, that shooting pain, that supreme summoning of resolution and fortitude. I had not seen her since the night of our vigil. She had kept strictly to her room.

I did not dare pause outside the door this time, lest my faltering limbs should fail me. I knew that once I was in the room strength would come. I went in.

She was not in her armchair, sitting at the big centre-table, as I expected. I had had a vision of myself once more running towards her, laying my head on her lap, kissing her hands.

No; she was standing in the bow-window, behind a smaller writing-table, where Signorina used to sit and do her accounts. In her hand, she held her long ivory paper-cutter. *Barricaded* flashed into my mind. She has barricaded and armed herself against me—I felt myself turn to steel.

"There's to be no scene, if you please, Olivia," she said coldly.

"I don't want to make a scene," I answered as coldly.

There was a long pause. She stood with her back towards me, looking out of the window. Then she began in a changed voice, as if she were talking to herself:

"It has been a struggle all my life—but I have always been victorious—I was proud of my victory." And then her voice changed, broke, deepened, softened, became a murmur: "I wonder now whether defeat wouldn't have been better for us all—as well as sweeter." Another long pause. She turned now and looked at me, and smiled. "You, Olivia, will never be victorious, but if you are defeated——" how she looked at me! "when you are defeated——" she looked at me in a way that made my heart stand still and the blood rush to my face, to my forehead, till I seemed to be wrapped in flame—then she suddenly broke off and brushed her hand across her eyes, as if brushing away an importunate vision. When I saw them again, they were extinguished and lifeless.

"I don't know what I'm saying," she went on dully. "I've got a headache. Good-bye."

I remained silent—rooted to the ground—uncomprehending—bewildered.

"Good-bye," she repeated angrily. I believe she stamped her foot. "Can't you understand? Good-bye."

I was dismissed. This was the end. But before I reached the door, she called again: "Olivia!"

Ah! she has relented! Ah! now I shall be gathered to her heart, and impatient as the wind, I turned to fly towards her—but she was still behind the table. Her attitude, her voice, her look, stern, hard and proud, put a still more impassable barrier between us.

"I had forgotten," she said, "that I must give you a parting present—a book—I think—but I don't know where it is——" She fingered vaguely some volumes that lay before her.

"Take this instead," she said and handed me across the table her long ivory paper-cutter. "And now send me the next girl."

Those were the last words I ever heard her speak: "And now send me the next girl."

I took the paper-cutter—a gift, I thought bitterly, that lessens no distance between us—that she can give me without any fear of our fingers touching. I left the room in a turmoil of resentment—hatred almost. This, then, was the end. No, no, it was impossible. Unbearable and therefore impossible. And yet I knew all the time that it was not only possible but that it must be borne. It was movement I wanted—to fling the crushing thought from my mind as a wild colt shakes off the intolerable, galling burden of a saddle. I rushed upstairs. I tore open the window and flung the paper-cutter out into the garden as far as I had strength to hurl. I seized a cloak and *bérêt* (all the time I was moving, I needn't be thinking) and ran downstairs. Out of the house, out of the grounds, across the road, into the forest, I ran. Mad thoughts pursued me—I fled from them as from relentless all-powerful enemies; mad dreams called to me—I ran towards them as to some miraculous saviour. I should meet her. She would step out from behind that tree—no, from behind the next—I should be in her arms once more—once more. We should be reconciled. I should understand at last. I could bear to say good-bye to her for ever, if only before the end, one moment of communion might be granted me. It would be. It must be. I ran till I was exhausted and breathless, knowing that when I stopped running that relentless enemy would be upon me, grinding me, torturing me. At last I could run no longer. I flung myself on the ground and buried my face in a heap of moss. No, no, that would never do, I must get up, I must walk. And now, I was as impatient to get back to the house as I had been to leave it. Perhaps something would have happened in the interval—perhaps—perhaps——

But when I got back everything was unchanged. No one had noticed my absence. I walked past the library—the door was open—it was empty—up again to my little room. The time had come. There was no more help for it. I must face it out.

I sat on my bed and tried to compose myself. And still, do what I would, hope came to interfere with my thoughts, my resolves. How hard it is to kill hope! Time after time, one thinks one has trodden it down, stamped it to death. Time after time, like a noxious insect, it begins to stir again, it shivers back again into a faint tremulous life. Once more it worms its way into one's heart, to instil its poison, to gnaw away the solid hard foundations of life and leave in their place the hollow phantom of illusion.

"She will come to see me to night," I thought. "I mustn't despair yet. To-night! To-night!" But how was I to get through the time till then? And if she didn't come—what then? What then?

I began tossing my things into my trunk, taking them out again and tossing them back. I was doing this, when Signorina came into my room.

"I've brought you a cup of tea," she said.

"Thank you, I don't want it," I answered, my head still in my trunk.

"Mlle Julie has gone to Paris——"

Hope! Hope!

"——she's not coming back to-night. She's spending the weekend with the R——s. You'd better drink your tea."

And she left the room.

Ha! That was better. The noxious creature was dead now. It would undermine me no longer. I was free at last from its insidious burrowings. I could be calm now and brace myself to endure.

I went to the window and looked out. I should never see that sky, those trees, that road again. The road along which I used to hear her carriage driving back at night. Good-bye! Good-bye! *Pour jamais adieu! Pour jamais!*

I knelt down by my bed and burst into tears.

XIV

THROUGHOUT the journey home and during many weeks, months and perhaps years, I pondered the episodes I have just related. I lived them over again, sometimes with ecstasy, sometimes with anguish. But more often I tried to think what had been the meaning of her attitude to me. As for those obscure words, spoken in our last interview, as I was standing silent before her, though now they seem to me to cast a curious illumination over the whole story, I barely remembered them. They were incomprehensible, and it was not of them I thought but of all the rest.

She had seemed to be fond of me. At moments I had dared to think she had loved me. Why had she treated me so at the end? Had I offended her? Had she changed? That was more probable. She had remembered that the only person she had ever loved was the dead woman on the bed. She hated me for having dared intrude into that privacy, for having thrust upon her a love she resented. But yet, I thought, why, why? Had I not been humble? Had I ever asked or wanted more than kindness? Had I ever dreamt that more was possible from her to me? Sometimes an uneasy conscience murmured "yes". She knew, she guessed perhaps the secret fluttering of my senses. Had she been disgusted? I put that dreadful thought away and began afresh. It was a scene she had dreaded. If I had gone into hysterics of tears, she might have broken down and wept too. But was I in the habit of having hysterics? It was unjust to think it. My tears were usually silent. And in any case, I thought angrily, she had no right to treat me with such cruelty, just to spare herself the inconvenience of my tears. She should have put up with them. Did she not owe me that at least? Perhaps, after all, she had left me with that last cruel memory out of some idea that it was for my good. Perhaps she had thought she would cure me in that way, that so I should suffer less. Oh, how mistaken! How dreadfully mistaken! She had not realized, she could not conceive the depth of the wound she had given me, how it had cut into the very quick of my life, how it had maimed me for ever. And such a little effort on her part, so small an exercise of her imagination, would have saved me, would have helped me to get through these dreary months and years. But why should she make an effort, even the smallest, for my sake? She didn't care. She didn't care. Her thoughts were elsewhere—with the past—with the future. I was nothing to her. Nothing. So, I consumed my heart with love and resentment, my eyes with hot, slow tears.

One day, I suddenly heard her voice as if she were speaking to me. A sentence came back to me I had forgotten. The voice said, earnestly, solemnly:

"Believe, Olivia, believe, I don't want to harm you."

There descended on me then a sudden and almost magic calm. Grace touched me mysteriously. The stifling, blinding clouds rolled away from my heart, from my eyes; I was able to breathe, to see once more. I was saved.

That night, I wrote her a letter. I told her that I had hated her, that that had been the worst of my pain, but that now I was reconciled to her, to life. I loved her again with all that was best in me. I was going to be happy; I was going to work, to live. I was going to try again.

I wrote by the same post to Signorina and begged for news.

Signorina had written to me once or twice. She had told me of their arrival in a big Canadian town, and of their settling into a small house. Mlle Julie had refused to start another school. They had enough to live on and were able to occupy themselves sufficiently. Signorina gave Italian lessons. Mlle

Julie was busy with translations. Short, dry letters. Signorina was no writer. But once she told me that the ivory paper-cutter had been found in the garden, and that Mlle Julie always used it.

Need I say, however, that the letter I longed for in answer to mine, the letter I hoped for, was to be from Mlle Julie? I dreamt of it. I wrote it in my head. It was to be tender and helpful. But it never came. It was only Signorina who wrote. I give her letter:

Olivia mia,

You ask for news. There isn't much to give you. There has been no particular change since last I wrote. Mlle Julie is well, but she still has fits of weeping. She had one the other day, and I knew it was because she had had a letter from you. I found the pieces in the waste-paper basket. Yesterday she said to me, "Tell Olivia not to write again." That was all.

As for me, I am happy. But you needn't mind. She doesn't care for me really, and when she comes to die, she will turn me out of her room and not allow me to come near her. I know that. In the meantime, I brush her hair and go on my knees before her and cut her nails. That is enough for me. It wouldn't be for you. Your share has been something more. But you have had to pay for it.

Addio.

Thank God that when that letter came, I was able to think of her and no longer of myself.

It was four years later that I got my last letter from Signorina.

Olivia mia,

Mlle Julie died last night of pneumonia. She wasn't ill long.

She was able to give me some few directions of what to do in case of her death and told me how to dispose of some of her belongings. She said I was to send you her ivory paper-cutter.

She has left me enough to live on. My mother and sister are coming to join me.

Addio.

The ivory paper-cutter is lying on my desk as I write this. It has her name engraved on it: JULIE.

AFTERWORD

IN February 1948 André Gide received an unusually
triumphant letter from his English translator. Used to hearing
about Gide's exploits, she now had "a little adventure of my
own" to confess. The manuscript of a story which she had sent to
Gide some fifteen years earlier—"Oh how could I be so
idiotic?"—and which Gide had stuffed in a desk drawer, had at
last been shown to friends in London. Rosamond Lehmann had
praised it; Leonard Woolf wanted to publish it. The story was
Olivia; the author, anonymous on publication in 1949, was
Dorothy Strachey Bussy, Lytton Strachey's sister.

It is not difficult to see why Dorothy Strachey chose to publish
anonymously. The main features of *Olivia* are autobiographical
and inflammatory. The headmistress to whom the narrator
becomes passionately attached is a thinly-disguised portrait of a
teacher Dorothy Strachey knew and admired; the home the
narrator leaves is clearly recognizable as the Strachey household.
The novel is a hymn of praise to one woman and the sensibility
she cultivated. It is also an act of defiance directed at the
Stracheys. Dorothy Strachey shared her brother's sense of
oppression at the "grim machine" of their Lancaster Gate home.
He anatomised its "dowdiness" and "foggy distances"; she wrote
disparagingly of its "solid comfort" and "ugly objects". He
noted with disdain his parents' "absence of nerves"; she observed
that her mother was "completely unaware of her senses". Both
showed a particular interest in a sister who had died in infancy.
This sister prompted some striking lines from the nine-year-old
Lytton:

To me Life is a burden
  But to thee
The joyous pleasures of the world
  Are all a gaiety.

Her name provided Dorothy Strachey with the title of this novel.

Olivia celebrates the narrator's release from the principled charmlessness of Lancaster Gate to places and people characterized as "exquisite", "ravishing", "delicious". It is a novel which exults in refinements of taste, in stolen kisses, in emotional susceptibility, and which creates a wholly feminine but hardly feminist world—a world of languishing and devoted tending, of flurry and fret and fragrant consolations. At its centre, in the figure of Mlle Julie, is the stylish and sceptical French schoolteacher whom Lytton Strachey called "cette grande femme".

Mlle Julie is a portrait of Marie Souvestre, who was the headmistress first of a school at Fontainebleau which Dorothy and her sister Elinor attended, later of a school in London where Dorothy taught. The energy, charm and literary flair ascribed to her in *Olivia* are amply affirmed by other admirers. Marie Souvestre was a friend of Leslie Stephen and John Morley; she was vehemently anti-religious and pro-Boer. Henry James declared that her school at "high, breezy Wimbledon" held "a very particular place"; Beatrice Webb thought her "a remarkable woman, with a gift of brilliant expression". Mrs Webb did, however, have some reservations, complaining that "an absence of humility ... narrowed her influence to those whom she happened to like and who happened to like her". There was a touch of Jean Brodie in Marie Souvestre, to which the cloistered intensities of *Olivia* bear witness. She had favourites among her pupils—Eleanor Roosevelt, Beatrice Chamberlain, Dorothy Strachey—and these favourites were treated to select readings in a library decorated with flowers and paintings by Puvis de Chavannes. Her girls were not encouraged to play games, but urged to lie down for an hour after lunch and consider a single thought, to be discussed, in French, at tea. Eleanor Roosevelt's schooling also included visits to the Comédie Française and a trip to Florence, where the pupil procured the hansoms and porters, and the headmistress selected the desirable sights. She was commended by Marie Souvestre for "a fineness of feeling truly exquisite"; her nail-biting was monitored by the headmistress's constant companion, the tiny and vigorous Mlle Samaia—*Olivia*'s Signorina.

It has been suggested that Eleanor Roosevelt, who was also praised by her teacher for "the perfect quality of her soul", is the altruistic and scholarly Laura of *Olivia*—a plausible notion, given Eleanor Roosevelt's success at Marie Souvestre's Wimbledon school. But it is at least as likely that Laura, who is described as being the daughter of "perhaps the most important man in England at the time", was Beatrice, the eldest daughter of Joseph Chamberlain and half-sister of Neville. Beatrice Chamberlain was a friend of the Strachey family: one of Lytton's earliest memories was of her "playing at having tea with me, with leaves and acorns, under a tree". She was older than Dorothy Strachey, as Laura is older than Olivia, and attended Marie Souvestre's school in France, not the later Wimbledon version—where Eleanor Roosevelt was taught by Dorothy Strachey. Like Laura, who is praised in *Olivia* for the generosity with which she welcomes the authority of a new stepmother, Beatrice Chamberlain had managed her father's household between his marriages. And Dorothy Strachey's Italian literary tendencies might well have inclined her to replace Dante's "Beatrice" with Petrarch's "Laura".

Laura's calm appreciation of Mlle Julie is contrasted with Olivia's frantic infatuation. Such fervour, and its attendant miseries, was not a feature only of Dorothy Strachey's adolescence. When she admired she adored. She needed heroes, and she loved where it was difficult or dangerous to love. Her marriage in 1903, when she was nearly forty, to the French painter Simon Bussy was described by Lytton Strachey as an act of "extraordinary courage" which shook the Strachey household. Lady Strachey, who might perhaps have preferred the suitor who became Chairman of the Board of Inland Revenue, thought that "the terrible feature" of the marriage was "the smallness of means"; her son grumbled more idiosyncratically about the couple's affectionateness: "Two people loving each other so much—there's something devilishly selfish about it."

Life at the Bussys' house in the South of France—where, Strachey wrote, "the pink of beauty reigns"—must have fulfilled many of the expectations of exquisiteness aroused by Marie Souvestre. But Dorothy Strachey still had room for a hero. In 1918 she met André Gide. She helped to teach him English, became his chief English translator, and began a correspondence with him which lasted until Gide's death thirty years later. Their letters—of which over a thousand survive—are of particular interest to a reader of *Olivia*. Gide valued Dorothy Strachey and the work she did; she was obsessed by him. She wrote to him about the task of translation, sounding, she remarked, as if she were giving "advice to the newly married": "Our chief merits must be first *Comprehension*—and then *respect, fidelity*, and *abnegation*." She also wrote about the "radiance of your presence" and "your essential beauty". She did so with little encouragement from Gide, who noted coolly that "the time will come, and soon—when your friendship can be a great support". The vocabulary of her unrequited adoration is familiar. In 1920, some twelve years before she began to describe gazing at the "great beauty" of Mlle Julie's "austere" forehead and lips, thinking, "she must have suffered," she was writing to Gide:

The things that make a face beautiful to me are the things that are pre-eminent in yours—thought and suffering and experience—knowledge of good and evil. Oh! how I like to look at your forehead and wonder and wonder what is working behind it ... and your lips, your lips, sweet, austere, incredibly mysterious ...

When Gide put *Olivia* into his desk drawer he may have been dismissing a love-letter addressed to him.

Susannah Clapp, London, 1987